IMAGES
of America

NORTH AUGUSTA
James U. Jackson's Dream

James U. Jackson

James U. Jackson, shown here in an etching, founded the city of North Augusta. (Courtesy North Augusta Historical Society.)

On the Cover: This automobile led the Fiftieth Anniversary Parade in 1956. The passengers in the back seat are, from left to right, James U. Jackson's daughter, Edith; his son, John; and his daughter, Daisy. (Courtesy Charles E. Petty.)

IMAGES
of America

NORTH AUGUSTA
James U. Jackson's Dream

Jeanne M. McDaniel
Foreword by
North Augusta Mayor Lark W. Jones

Published by Arcadia Publishing
Charleston, South Carolina

Library of Congress Catalog Card Number: 2005927743

For all general information contact Arcadia Publishing at:
Telephone 843-853-2070
Fax 843-853-0044
E-mail sales@arcadiapublishing.com
For customer service and orders:
Toll-Free 1-888-313-2665

Visit us on the Internet at www.arcadiapublishing.com

To the citizens of North Augusta,
who have the vision to perpetuate the dream,
and to the Heritage Council of North Augusta
and its efforts to preserve our history and heritage.

CONTENTS

FOREWORD

Having lived in North Augusta my entire life and being a student of history, I knew James U. Jackson as the "Founder of North Augusta." In this detailed account of his life by Jeanne McDaniel, I have learned that he was so much more. To know a person, you need to look at his or her family background and heritage. James U. Jackson's success was remarkable given the ups and downs of his father, the death of his first wife at age 26, and the death of an infant child, not to mention the time required to stay on top of all his varied business interests. This offering provides a close look at the many sides of Jackson. Whether it was forming a new railroad, operating a brokerage business, forming the North Augusta Land Company, constructing the Thirteenth Street Bridge, creating an electric trolley line, or building the Hampton Terrace Hotel, Jackson may have been the founder of not only the town of North Augusta but the "Mega Conglomerate Company."

Jackson's contributions to North Augusta have shaped the past and have helped form our future. His Rosemary Hall, along with Lookaway Hall built by his brother, Walter, has been a landmark in the center of town. His land plan of the original city showed a vision with principles that are highly respected and regularly used over a hundred years later.

I believe that James U. Jackson would be pleased if he visited North Augusta today. He would be pleased not only with the physical aspects and growth of North Augusta, but also with her people and her sense of community. He would be proud to know that his influence is still felt today.

"Why doesn't someone build a town on the hill across the river?" was the question Jackson asked as a youngster. He had the vision and the ability to do it. Thousands of lives are richer because he did. Thanks to North Augustan Jeanne McDaniel for her time, talent, and effort in bringing his story to us.

Mayor Lark W. Jones
City of North Augusta

ACKNOWLEDGMENTS

George Jackson and Donna Alexander collection of family memorabilia

Gordon A. Blaker, Augusta Museum of History

Emily Boyles, Tuttle-Newton Home, Augusta

Hazel Jackson Boyles collection of family memorabilia

Stan Byrdy, Augusta sports historian

Melody Carter, Wachovia Bank

Dr. Edward J. Cashin, Center for the Study of Georgia History, Augusta State University

Sandra L. Croy, Rosemary and Lookaway Halls, North Augusta

Joyce Davis, Kristi Deason, and Janice Farr

Victoria Hann and staff, Greater North Augusta Chamber of Commerce

Linda Harless, Julia Holiday, Scott McPherson, and Mattison Verdery

Dr. Joe Holt, Pine Heights, North Augusta

Mayor Lark W. Jones and staff, City of North Augusta

Adam Ferrell, Adam Latham, and Laura New, Arcadia Publishing

Joseph M. Lee III, personal collection, postcards

Judy McAlhany, Augusta–Richmond County Historical Society, Reese Library, Augusta State University

Nelson Morgan, and Steven Brown, Hargrett Rare Book and Manuscript Library, University of Georgia Libraries

Jerry W. Murphy, Magnolia Cemetery, Augusta

Milledge G. Murray, personal collection, Augusta history

John J. O'Shea and Carol Waggoner-Angleton, Special Collections, Reese Library, Augusta State University

John Paul and Robert G. Croom, Heritage Council of North Augusta

Charles E. Petty collection of photographs

Dayton Sherrouse, Amy Priessmann, and Rebecca B. Rogers, Augusta Canal Authority

INTRODUCTION

This is the story of a man, his family, and his dream. It is impossible to separate the story of James U. Jackson from the story of North Augusta and its development. I hope the reader will indulge the writer when the facts and photographs from familiar sources are included as part of this story. As with all history, however many times a story is told, one can find differences in the views of each storyteller. These differences in perspective prompt the reader to want to learn more about the subject; thus the writer has achieved her goal, stimulating an interest. We have a need to learn more about those who walked these streets before us and the dream that carries us all forward to a greater tomorrow. I have used a number of published sources for both facts and photographs, and gratefully acknowledge them all. I am heavily indebted to all of these sources. As a member of the Heritage Council of North Augusta, I was more than happy to write this story. I sincerely hope the reader receives as much enjoyment as the writer as the story of James Urquhart Jackson, founder of the city of North Augusta, is recounted here.

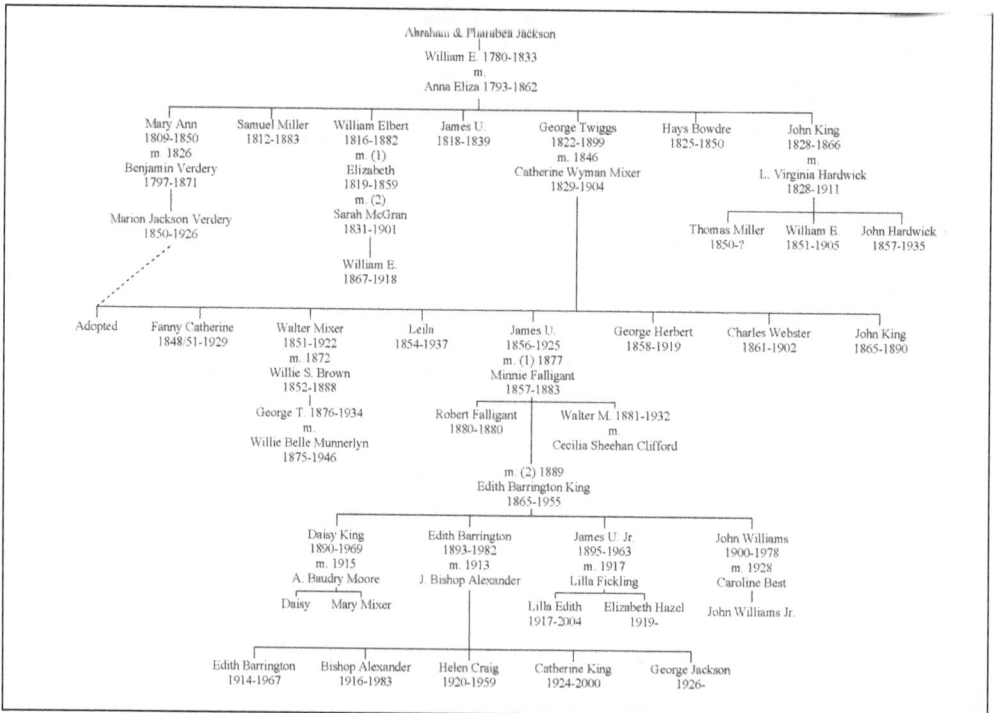

Abraham & Pharabea Jackson

William E. 1780-1833
m.
Anna Eliza 1793-1862

Mary Ann 1809-1850 m. 1826 Benjamin Verdery 1797-1871	Samuel Miller 1812-1883	William Elbert 1816-1882 m. (1) Elizabeth 1819-1859 m. (2) Sarah McGran 1831-1901	James U. 1818-1839	George Twiggs 1822-1899 m. 1846 Catherine Wyman Mixer 1829-1904	Hays Bowdre 1825-1850	John King 1828-1866 m. L. Virginia Hardwick 1828-1911

Marion Jackson Verdery 1850-1926

William E. 1867-1918

Thomas Miller 1850-?	William E. 1851-1905	John Hardwick 1857-1935

Adopted	Fanny Catherine 1848/51-1929	Walter Mixer 1851-1922 m. 1872 Willie S. Brown 1852-1888	Leila 1854-1937	James U. 1856-1925 m. (1) 1877 Minnie Falligant 1857-1883	George Herbert 1858-1919	Charles Webster 1861-1902	John King 1865-1890

George T. 1876-1934
m.
Willie Belle Munnerlyn 1875-1946

Robert Falligant 1880-1880	Walter M. 1881-1932 m. Cecilia Sheehan Clifford

m. (2) 1889
Edith Barrington King 1865-1955

Daisy King 1890-1969 m. 1915 A. Baudry Moore	Edith Barrington 1893-1982 m. 1913 J. Bishop Alexander	James U. Jr. 1895-1963 m. 1917 Lilla Fickling	John Williams 1900-1978 m. 1928 Caroline Best

Daisy	Mary Mixer		

Lilla Edith 1917-2004	Elizabeth Hazel 1919-	John Williams Jr.

Edith Barrington 1914-1967	Bishop Alexander 1916-1983	Helen Craig 1920-1959	Catherine King 1924-2000	George Jackson 1926-

8

One

THE JACKSON FAMILY
1830–1856

Named for an uncle who died of yellow fever in 1839 at the age of 20, James Urquhart Jackson was born in the village of Harrisonville, Georgia, on June 24, 1856. Harrisonville was located in the area of today's Fifteenth Street and Wrightsboro Road in present-day Augusta, Georgia. The founder of the city of North Augusta first dreamed of a community on the hill above the Savannah River as a young boy. Looking north across the river from Augusta, James U. Jackson asked his father, George Twiggs Jackson, why no one had ever developed the area. "No one has ever had the vision, my son," was said to have been his father's reply. The younger Jackson vowed he would build a city there. A little more than 20 years later, his dream began to take shape.

James's father, George, attended the Academy of Richmond County. He was a shrewd businessman and an indomitable force in Augusta business. Involved in railroads, mills, and banking for more than 30 years, George T. and an older brother, William E., were on the boards of many companies during the last half of the 19th century. In 1830, the South Carolina Railroad Company began to build the first steam-operated railroad to carry the U.S. mail and offer regular passenger service. Opened in 1833, the line was 136 miles long and connected Hamburg, a community close to today's Fifth Street Bridge area in North Augusta, and Charleston, South Carolina.

The Georgia Railroad was chartered in the same year by the state legislature to build a railroad west from Augusta. Two years later, the charter was amended to grant the company banking powers and change the name to the Georgia Railroad and Banking Company. In 1841, the headquarters of the banking operations was moved from Athens to Augusta. That same year, James U. Jackson's grandparents, William E. and Ann Eliza Jackson, were living on Center Street (today's Fifth Street) between Ellis and Greene Streets. The family business was located at 266 Broad Street.

A faded and difficult-to-read entry in the Jackson family Bible shows William E. Jackson's parents were Abraham and Pharabea Jackson. George Twiggs Jackson, James U. Jackson's father, had several siblings. Among them was John King Jackson, who became a lawyer and later a distinguished general in the War Between the States. He fought at the battles of Shiloh, Chickamauga, and Chattanooga, among others. He returned to Augusta and the practice of law after the war. An advertisement in the *Augusta Chronicle* informed the public that he had resumed his practice and was located at the Masonic Building, in the office of his brother, George T. Sadly, while on a business trip to Milledgeville in 1866, he became ill and died of pneumonia at the age of 38. He is buried in the Magnolia Cemetery in Augusta.

Another of George T.'s siblings, older brother William Elbert, was active in commerce all his working life. He and James U.'s father were partners in George T. Jackson and Company as stock and bond brokers. He was president of the National Bank of Augusta and president of the Augusta Factory from its reorganization in 1858–1859 until his death in 1882.

An older sister of William E. and George T., Mary Ann, had married Benjamin Francis Verdery in 1826. They had 12 children, three of whom died in infancy. Tragically, in 1850, five days after the birth of a son, Marion Jackson Verdery, Mary died. Marion Jackson was taken to his grandmother to be cared for and was later adopted by his uncle, George Twiggs, James U.'s father. Thus, a long association began between James and his cousin and adopted brother, Marion Jackson Verdery. The two well-established families of the Jacksons and the Verderys lived on adjacent properties in Augusta and had close business ties throughout their adult lives. Marion Jackson Verdery died in 1926, a year after James U. Jackson.

In 1845, the Georgia Railroad line to Marthasville was completed. Marthasville, known earlier as Terminus, is known today as Atlanta, capital of the state of Georgia. The Georgia Railroad and Banking Company helped finance a waterpower canal system to establish Augusta as an important manufacturing center. Augusta is considered to be the birthplace of the Southern textile mills. The Augusta Canal Company was formed in 1845 as a publicly owned corporation to handle the financing and construction of the Augusta Canal System. Col. Henry Cumming was the president of the new company. It is possible that Whig presidential candidate Henry Clay first mentioned the idea of a canal during a visit to Judge Henry Warren in 1844. Judge Warren owned property around Rock Creek and Lake Warren. Eli Whitney's cotton gin was first operated in the area at Rock Creek. Most of the laborers who worked on the canal were slaves. There were crews that probably included freed blacks and Irish workers. The first water flowed through the gates in November 1846 into the first level of the canal, which was seven miles long and five feet deep. It was capable of producing 600 horsepower for industry. The following month, George Twiggs Jackson married Catherine Wyman Mixer at the U.S. Hotel, home of her father, Daniel Mixer, on December 15, 1846. The completion of the canal a year later had a profound effect on Augusta. The Augusta Factory was organized in 1847. It was located at Fenwick Street and Marbury Street (today's Twelfth Street). In 1848, the second and third levels of the canal were completed, bringing it to nine miles in length. The Granite Mill was built at this time and is the only mill along the original canal that is still standing. By 1850, 25,000 bales of cotton annually were being transported down the river on Petersburg boats, loaded onto wagons, and taken to market.

The census of 1850 lists James U. Jackson's and Marion Jackson Verdery's grandmother as a 54-year-old widow living at the family home in Harrisonville. Other members of the household were 33-year-old William E., his 30-year-old wife Elizabeth, and their two children, 12-year-old Mary and 10-year-old Andrew. George Twiggs, 27, and his wife, Catherine, 22, are listed as having a child, one-year-old Frances. Also at the Harrisonville address is younger brother Hays Bowdre, who died shortly after at the age of 25. The Jackson property in Harrisonville was comprised of more than one house on several lots in the general area of what is today the intersection of Wrightsboro Road and Fifteenth Street. Today Poplar Street is around the center of the Jackson property. The Verdery properties were significantly larger in area. Verdery Street can be found today between Central Avenue and Wrightsboro Road, from Wilson to Fifteenth Street. Florence and Twelfth (Marbury) Streets cross near the center of the Verdery territory.

Cousins and brothers by adoption, James U. and Marion Jackson were six years apart in age. When James graduated from the University of Georgia in 1876, he and Marion began a brokerage company, Verdery and Jackson. They remained close business associates all their lives. Marion Jackson Verdery, after working for Augusta papers and as a stock and bond broker in partnership with James U. Jackson, moved to New York. He earned a living writing for various publications, then moved back into the brokerage business.

Fearing loss of status as a commercial center, Augusta had resisted connecting the rail lines on the Georgia side of the Savannah River with the South Carolina Railway Company. Finally, after Charleston threatened to plan to cross the river elsewhere, Augusta agreed, and the South Carolina Railway crossed the Savannah River in 1853.

At the time of Jackson's birth in 1856, his father was a director of the Georgia Railroad and Banking Company. He had been elected to that position in 1854 and remained on the board until 1882. While serving on the board, he promoted the building of the Port Royal and Augusta Railroad and the Charlotte, Columbia, and Augusta Railroads, among many other endeavors.

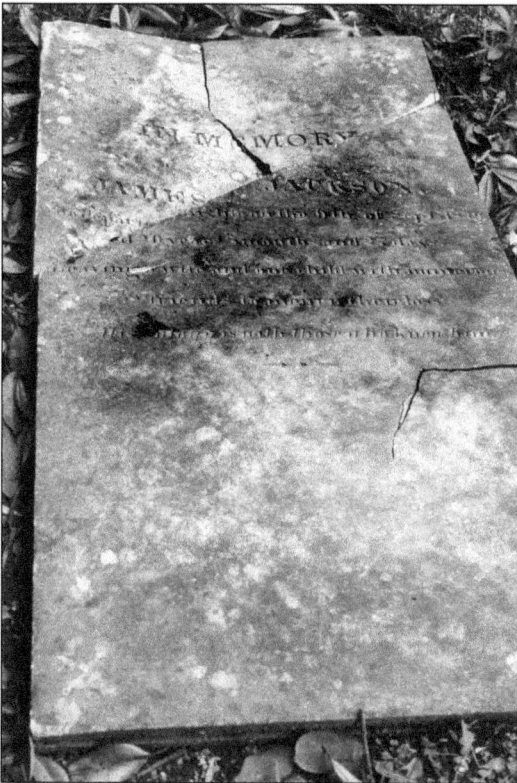

James Urquhart Jackson was named for an uncle who died of yellow fever in 1839. His uncle is buried in the Magnolia Cemetery in Augusta. (Courtesy Heritage Council of North Augusta.)

James U. Jackson was probably in his mid-30s at the time this portrait was made. In other images from the late 19th century to early 20th century, Jackson is seen sporting a walrus moustache in this portrait. (Courtesy Hazel Jackson Boyles.)

This portrait is of George Twiggs Jackson (1822–1899). He was president of the Enterprise Manufacturing Company, from its organization in 1877 until 1884. A reversal of fortune in 1884 caused he and his family great pain. The date of this portrait is not known, but George T. Jackson appears to be middle aged. It could have been 1872 when he was one of the incorporators of the City Loan and Savings Bank. (Courtesy Hazel Jackson Boyles.)

A historic marker for the South Carolina Railroad can be found on the side of Highway 1/78 at the bottom of the ramp as one travels south on Martintown Road. (Courtesy Heritage Council of North Augusta.)

The *Best Friend of Charleston*, shown here, was destroyed in 1831 by a boiler explosion shortly after being put into service. However, it proved the practicality of a steam locomotive and that a steel wheel on an iron rail was a viable mode of travel. It helped to develop the port of Charleston with the transportation of goods and passengers. (Courtesy North Augusta Historical Society.)

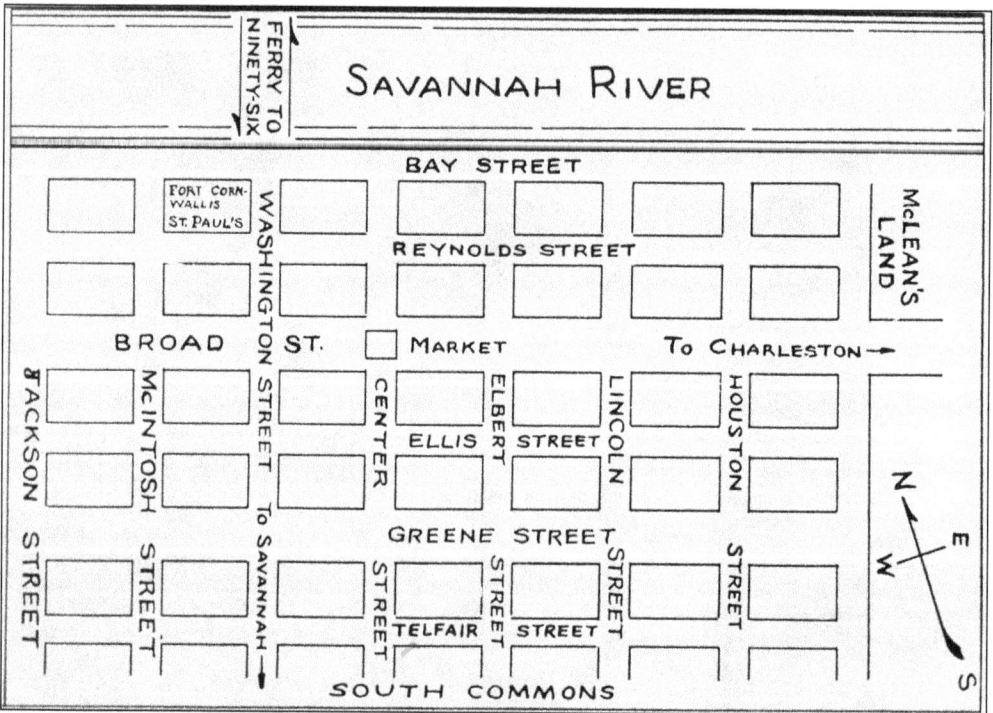

The streets in this 1780 map of Augusta are identified by names used at the time. Some street signs today reflect the present and the earlier names used. For example, Marbury street is known today as Twelfth Street, and similarly, today's Eighth Street was once named Jackson Street. (Courtesy Richmond County Historical Society, Reese Library, Augusta State University.)

Shown here is the Jackson family Bible. There are some family entries in the Bible, but it does not provide a complete family history. (Courtesy George Jackson Alexander.)

Gen. John King Jackson is buried in the Magnolia Cemetery in Augusta. He was an uncle of James U. Jackson and a younger brother of James's father, George T. Jackson. An attorney before the War Between the States, Gen. John King Jackson fought at the battles of Shiloh, Chickamunga, Chattanooga, and others. He resumed the practice of law after the war and died suddenly of pneumonia at the age of 38 in 1866. (Courtesy Heritage Council of North Augusta.)

William Elbert Jackson, an uncle of James U. Jackson, was a major force in Augusta business and politics in the mid- to late 19th century. His grave, pictured here, can be found in the Magnolia Cemetery in Augusta. (Courtesy Heritage Council of North Augusta.)

This sketch depicts an early train to Marthasville (Atlanta) on the Georgia Railroad. The sketch is included in an anniversary booklet given to customers in 1983 to celebrate the 150th anniversary of the First Railroad and Banking Company of Georgia. The wood burning locomotive *Florida* arrived in Marthasville (Atlanta) in 1842, hauled overland on a wagon from Madison by a 16 mule team. The city of Terminus became known as Marthasville (named for the daughter of Gov. Wilson Lumpkin) December 23, 1843. On December 29, 1845, it became known as Atlanta.

The locations of the Augusta Factory and the Jackson and Verdery properties are shown on this 1875 map of Augusta. (Courtesy Special Collections, Reese Library, Augusta State University.)

The Granite Mill is the only mill along the original Augusta Canal that is still standing. It can be seen at the canal side of the Enterprise Mill. Near the roofline is the date of 1848. (Photograph. Heritage Council of North Augusta. Courtesy Augusta Canal Authority.)

The Phinizy Mill at Rock Creek is where Eli Whitney's cotton gin was first operated in the local area. Whitney invented the cotton gin while he was at Mulberry Plantation near Savannah, Georgia, and patented it later. Eli Whitney made no profit from his invention. (Courtesy Milledge G. Murray Collection.)

Augusta resisted for years, but finally, in 1853, the bridge shown here was completed to connect the South Carolina Railroad with Georgia. (Courtesy Special Collections, Reese Library, Augusta State University.)

Two

THE JOURNEY BEGINS
1857–1889

The Jackson home in Harrisonville was described as the house on Fifteenth Street with 15 servants. There was a butler, two house servants, four servants, two gardeners, a cook, and a washerwoman—a total of 11, although there was probably more domestic help from time to time.

James had an older brother, Walter Mixer Jackson, some five years his senior, and two older sisters, Fanny, who never married, and Leila, who married Charles B. F. Lowe. Two younger brothers were George Herbert, born in 1858, and Charles Webster, born in 1861, as the War Between the States began. Born at the end of the conflict in 1865 was John King, who died as a young man in 1890. Of the nine children born to George Twiggs Jackson and Catherine Wyman Mixer Jackson, six survived to adulthood. Other than cousin and adopted brother Marion Jackson Verdery, only his two sisters outlived James. He and his brothers were associated with various business enterprises throughout their working lives.

When the Augusta Factory was reorganized in 1858–1859, James U. Jackson's uncle William E. became its president. His first wife, Elizabeth, died shortly after.

In 1858, the future president of the United States, Thomas Woodrow Wilson, came to live with his family in Augusta. Rev. Joseph R. Wilson, Woodrow Wilson's father, was pastor of the First Presbyterian Church on Telfair Street in Augusta from 1858 to 1870. The Jackson family was associated with the First Presbyterian Church for many years. It is noteworthy to reflect on the futures of both Woodrow Wilson and James U. Jackson, as they lived somewhat parallel lives in Augusta. They were born in the same year of 1856, and Thomas Woodrow Wilson died in 1924, the year before Jackson's life ended. Rev. Joseph R. Wilson conducted Gen. John King Jackson's funeral service in 1866 at the First Presbyterian Church.

Jackson's father, George Twiggs Jackson, remained with George T. Jackson and Company while George's younger brother, John King, worked as an attorney. John King and his wife, Virginia Hardwick, had three sons, Thomas Miller, William Elbert, and John Hardwick, who were 11, 9, and 5 years old as the War Between the States began in 1861. As contemporaries,

James and his cousins were closely associated in business as adults.

President of the Confederacy Jefferson Davis ordered Col. George Washington Rains to locate a suitable site for a Confederate powder works. Augusta was the site chosen because of the canal and the railroads. The powder works operated from 1862 to 1865. The chimney remains today. It serves as a monument to part of Augusta's history.

During the war in 1862, George T. opened a Poor Store on Broad and Washington Streets (today's Sixth Street). The Purveying Association helped the families of soldiers by supplying goods at a cut rate and provided a soup house. George's brother, William E., gave funds and donated cloth from the Augusta Factory. In 1863, 1,200 men turned out to defend Augusta if needed. One hundred men joined the Augusta Volunteers under Capt. George T. Jackson. He was one of those called upon to organize the men into a disciplined fighting force. At one time, it was reported that raiders were in Lincoln County heading toward Augusta. The report, however, proved to be a false alarm. Augusta avoided any major impact during the war years. During those years, George T. Jackson purchased the Coleman Granite Mill and became the head of the firm of Jackson, Miller, and Verdery with associates John T. Miller and Edward F. Kinchley in the flour and grain business.

As Augusta undertook to rebuild its economy after the war, James U. Jackson's uncle, William E., was a city council member and loaned the city $7,500 to help in rebuilding the economy. After the war, the city of Augusta began to grow and prosper. John King Jackson returned from active duty and resumed the practice of law until his untimely death in 1866. James's father and his uncle William E. were two of the incorporators of the National Bank of Augusta and the Mechanics Savings Bank. The two brothers were associated with many Augusta businesses. George T. was a director of the Georgia Railroad and Banking Company in 1866. Col. George Washington Rains urged city council to enlarge the canal in June 1869. He reported in June of the following year the work could be done for $500,000. Mayor Charles Estes arranged for Charles Olmstead, who had been an engineer on the Erie Canal, to come to Augusta. Both Olmstead and the city engineer did a survey and reported the cost of the enlargement would be $371,000. Everyone was delighted, and voters approved the project. Plans were made immediately for the expected growth. Oglethorpe Manufacturing Company was the first factory organized. Among its list of founders and directors was George Twiggs Jackson. In October 1871, the city purchased the confiscated powder works property from the U.S. government. The total cost for the over 130 acres was $10,300. Changes in taxation on those investing in cotton and woolen mills were enacted. The Augusta Cotton Exchange was organized, and a building was constructed at Reynolds Street and Jackson Street (today's Eighth Street). Bales of cotton were unloaded from boats, put on wagons, and taken to Cotton Row daily.

Though most of the family remained in Harrisonville, James's uncle William E. lived with his wife and children on Greene Street. He remained as president of the Augusta Factory until his death in 1882. James's cousin, William E., was employed by the C. H. Phinizy. Cousin Andrew worked for Claghorn and Herring. James's older brother, Walter, worked with his father at George T. Jackson and Company. In 1872, George T. was one of the incorporators of the City Loan and Savings Bank.

While James Jackson was attending the Academy of Richmond County, as his father had before him, the enlargement of the Augusta Canal took place between 1872 and 1875. Four hundred workers were employed on the enlargement of the canal. Contractors brought in 200 Chinese laborers, half the total force. Many of these settled in the community. Olmstead decided it would be more cost effective to fill in the huge tunnels under the aqueduct; this effectively dammed Rae's Creek, creating Lake Olmstead. The final cost of the project was $920,000, almost triple the original Olmstead estimate.

Unable to pay a $40,000 loan, the canal company forfeited their property to the city. Although the Oglethorpe Company was re-chartered as the Cumming Manufacturing Company by the legislature, it was unable to attract investors and failed. In 1873, the year Lake Olmstead was created, James Jackson left the Academy of Richmond County and entered the University of

Georgia as a sophomore. In 1875, the year before he graduated from the University of Georgia and 10 years after the end of the War Between the States, his father was presented with a cane inscribed, "George T. Jackson OIC Co. 13 Nov. 17, 1875."

In this same year, Jackson was admitted to the First Presbyterian Church of Augusta on profession of faith. As an alumnus of the University of Georgia, he completed a questionnaire in 1901. It stated he graduated with speakers place in one of two degrees and was a senior debater Phi Kappa Society. Under the military heading, he stated he was sergeant his sophomore year, battalion color sergeant his junior year, captain his senior year, and orderly sergeant of the Richmond Hussars. He graduated with honors in 1876 with a bachelor's degree and immediately went into partnership with Marion Jackson Verdery as stock and bond brokers. His debating skills would serve him well throughout his business life.

The year of James Jackson's graduation from the University of Georgia, his father decided to take advantage of the increase in waterpower produced by the enlarged canal. He contacted Jones Davis, mill superintendent of Holyoke, Massachusetts, and the Enterprise Manufacturing Company was organized in March of the following year. With George T. as president of the Enterprise Manufacturing Company, the Granite Mill was purchased and became part of the new enterprise. As the first business on the newly enlarged canal, it is interesting to see it today, refurbished as offices and condominiums. Enterprise Mill in the 21st century retains the building's link with history. There is an Augusta Canal Interpretive center, and boat tours of the canal are conducted by the Augusta Canal Authority using reproductions of the Petersburg boats used for the movement of goods on the waterway more than 100 years ago.

On November 6, 1877, James U. Jackson married Minnie Falligant in Athens, Georgia. He and his wife lived with the family in Harrisonville. James and Minnie had two sons. Walter Marion was born in 1881 and died in 1932. The older son, Robert Falligant Jackson, died tragically of cholera in 1880 when he was just five months old. James's father was at the Enterprise Mill with son, Walter, while still remaining at George T. Jackson and Company. George T. continued on the board of directors of the Georgia Railroad and Banking Company. Uncle William remained as president of the Augusta Factory and the National Bank of Augusta. Cousin William, son of Gen. John King Jackson, was an attorney, as his father had been.

The enlarged deeper canal was the pride of the city; rowing races were held there. N. W. Armstrong, a bookkeeper at the Enterprise, ran a one-horsepower steamboat taking visitors on trips along the canal, hoping to interest them to invest in the new mills. In 1880, under the chairmanship of Josiah Sibley, the incorporators of the Sibley Manufacturing Company met, William E. Jackson was among the incorporators. Josiah Sibley had been a merchant in Augusta and Hamburg since 1821 and was the founder of the Langley Mill in 1870. Half of the $500,000 capital was raised in Augusta, and Josiah and his son William secured the balance in Cincinnati and New York. James's older brother Walter and his father became the proprietors of the Excelsior Flour Mill. His brother, George Herbert, worked with their father at the Enterprise Manufacturing Company. Due to George Twigg's planning, the Enterprise Manufacturing Company's first floor held 242 looms, the second floor had 14 British carding machines, and 10 "mule" spinning frames were on the third floor. The mill had begun operations in March 1878 and produced sheeting valued at over $42,000 in the first six months. Stockholders voted a 10 percent dividend.

By the summer of 1881, work was almost complete on the Sibley Mill. Augusta mayor Charles Estes went to New York and Boston with James Verdery to look for investors as the King Manufacturing Company was incorporated. James U. Jackson was prominent in the organization of the John P. King Manufacturing Company. The Sibley Mill was completed in September, and a row of two-story brick row houses for workers was built, with more planned.

By 1882, with his father as president of the Enterprise Mill and head of George T. Jackson and Company where brothers Charles W. and George Herbert worked, James remained associated with Marion Jackson Verdery as a stock and bond broker. This was the year of the death of his uncle, William Elbert, who had been so influential in the commerce of Augusta. George T., as a member of the building committee at the First Presbyterian Church, laid the cornerstone of the Telfair Building, Sunday School House, and library. These were demolished in 1976 as part of a building program.

The family was living together at Harrisonville with patriarch George T. His sons and nephews were associated with various businesses, including mills and banking. Sisters-in-law and grandchildren were all part of the extended family. Life was good for the Jacksons; not everything remained the same in Harrisonville, however. In December 1883, James's wife, Minnie Falligant Jackson, died. She was only 26 years old.

James Jackson began a business as a securities broker in 1884, negotiating many issues of railroad bonds. In October that year, George T. Jackson and Company declared bankruptcy, and in December the stockholders learned that their company was more than $200,000 in debt. At the same time, Roberts and Company, O'Donnell and Burke, and the Bank of Augusta all failed. George T. blamed the losses on the national slowdown. An investigation into the chain of failures revealed George T. Jackson—captain and later major of the Augusta volunteers during the War Between the States and businessman extraordinaire—stood accused of embezzling more than $250,000. The charge was that, as president of the Enterprise Mill in November 1882, he did embezzle, steal, and fraudulently take $117,667. In 1885, William Roberts, president of the Bank of Augusta and head of Roberts and Company, was indicted for grand larceny. He attempted suicide by slitting his throat, but he recovered. At the trial, Enterprise Company bookkeeper N. W. Armstrong, who had conducted the sightseeing trips on the newly enlarged canal, produced checks that George Twiggs had ordered destroyed. George T. Jackson pled not guilty and made a touching but fruitless speech stating that he intended to pay the money back. Although he was always a persuasive speaker, the checks produced by Armstrong left the verdict in little doubt. George Twiggs Jackson remained stoic as he was sentenced to six years in the penitentiary. His sons, son-in-law, and nephews were in court for him. As the verdict was pronounced, they bowed their heads and wept. George T. was pardoned after serving two years. In explaining his actions, he again made references to a general business slump.

In its first year, King Mill lost almost $30,000, and many mills were forced to slow production and lay off workers. Francis Cogin took over management of the Enterprise during the crisis. The company issued $250,000 in new stock to cover the losses. As the general business slump improved, workers began to demand more pay and better working conditions. In 1886, there was a strike at the Augusta Factory. When workers were threatened with eviction from mill housing, they went back to work.

James U. Jackson became vice president and later president of the Marietta and North Georgia Railroad while continuing as a stock and bond broker. He and other family members remained at the family home in Harrisonville. James P. Verdery was elected president of the Enterprise Company by the stockholders. In 1888, he added a weaving room to the factory; the mill soon became profitable again. James Jackson's brother, Charles Webster, was associated with C. W. Jackson grocers, and his youngest brother, John K., was with him, as was older brother, Walter M., as bookkeeper. Gen. John K. Jackson's widow and son, William E., an attorney, were living with the family in Harrisonville. After James Jackson's uncle, William E., died in 1882, his widow and son, William E., continued to live at the Greene Street house. William E. was working as a salesman with J. M. Burdell.

James Jackson was associated with a Tennessee railroad and the Augusta Southern Railroad. He was instrumental in broadening the narrow-gauge line to standard gauge. Later it became a trunk line of the Georgia and Florida Railroad. He continued as a stock and bond broker. With all his business responsibilities and community and family concerns, he still found time to relax and play a little baseball.

In 1888, James U. Jackson was the key to the organization of the Augusta National Exposition and was responsible for the outfitting of a rail car for tours and advertising. The Augusta Exposition was a major event for several years. In 1891, former-president Rutherford B. Hayes was a guest, as were ex-confederates John B. Gordon, Wade Hampton, and Joe Wheeler.

In October 1888, Jackson advertised his brokerage business at 729 Broad Street. His business associates were Marion Jackson Verdery and other New York and Southern financiers. As George Twiggs Jackson's star dimmed, his son's shone brightly in the world of commerce. On March 19, 1889, the widowed James married Edith Barrington King of Savannah. Together they had four children—two sons and two daughters. Edith was the daughter of a prominent Presbyterian minister. Habersham Street in Savannah takes its name from her mother's family—she was a descendant of the early Georgia governor James Habersham.

Jim Jackson resigned from the Marietta and North Georgia Railroad in 1889. Mill workers went on strike and were evicted from mill housing. George T. was back with the extended family at Harrisonville. Most records of the time give little notice to female family members. Sara, William E.'s second wife, and Virginia, who had been married to Gen. John King Jackson, seem to be the exception by virtue of their status as widows. James's sister, Leila, returned to the family home when she became a widow in 1892. Several family members were working in the grocery business.

With the railroads came easier, faster travel, and many people from the North came south to escape harsher climates. An entirely new industry evolved—the resort hotel. James U. Jackson was one of the organizers of the Bon Air Hotel in Augusta, which opened in August 1889.

Here is the Jackson home in the village of Harrisonville. Harrisonville no longer exists; it was in the area of Wrightsboro Road and Fifteenth Street. (Courtesy Catherine Harn Whitley.)

Canal Augusta Factory, Augusta, Ga.

The Augusta Factory was reorganized in 1858–1859. James U. Jackson's uncle, William E. Jackson, became its president at that time and remained in that position until his death in 1882. (Courtesy Special Collections, Reese Library, Augusta State University.)

This is the grave of William E. Jackson's first wife, Elizabeth, who died as her husband became president of the Augusta Factory. (Courtesy Heritage Council of North Augusta.)

Pres. Thomas Woodrow Wilson lived in this house from 1858 until 1870, when his father, Rev. Joseph R. Wilson, was the pastor of the First Presbyterian Church on Telfair Street. (Courtesy Heritage Council of North Augusta.)

This is the First Presbyterian Church on Telfair Street in Augusta today. (Courtesy Heritage Council of North Augusta.)

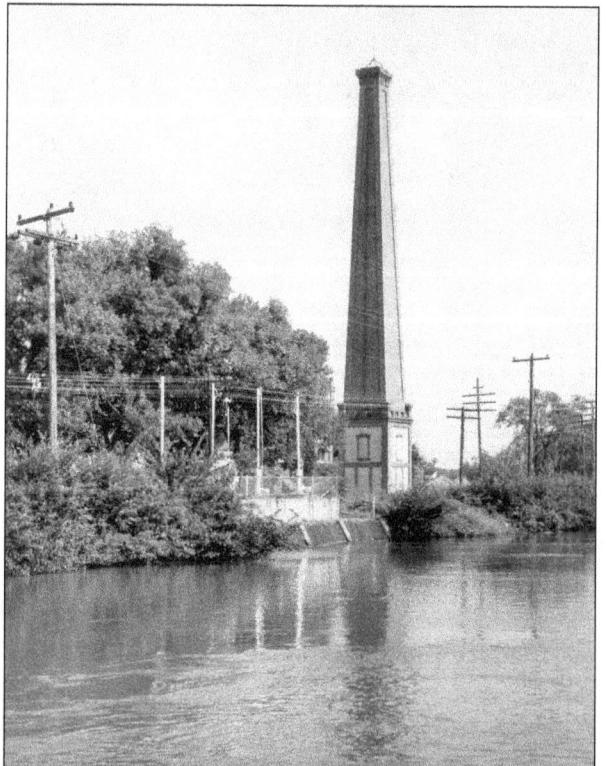

The chimney of the Confederate Powder Works remains today as a part of Augusta history. The powder works operated from 1862 until 1865. (Courtesy Special Collections, Reese Library, Augusta State University.)

The Coleman Granite Mill was purchased by James U. Jackson's father, George T. Jackson, during the War Between the States. It later became a part of the Enterprise Mill. (Courtesy Augusta Museum of History.)

CHARLES ESTES
BORN FEB. 2, 1818 AT CAPE VINCENT, N.Y.
BECAME A RESIDENT OF AUGUSTA, GA.
OCT. 1844, WHERE HE DIED MAR. 25, 1917
MAYOR OF THE CITY
FROM DEC. 1870 TO DEC. 1873

Charles Estes was mayor of Augusta during a pivotal time in the city's history. He is buried in the Magnolia Cemetery in Augusta adjacent to the monument and family graves of William E. Jackson. (Courtesy Heritage Council of North Augusta.)

The Cotton Exchange was located at Eighth (Jackson) and Reynolds Streets. Cotton Row was the scene for wagons hauling bales of cotton. Trade information on other goods was also available, quotations were recorded on grain, meat, and coffee from Chicago and New York as were the latest returns from the New York stock markets. (Courtesy Milledge G. Murray Collection.)

The Cotton Exchange Building today is home to the Georgia Bank and Trust Company. (Courtesy Heritage Council of North Augusta.)

Bales of cotton were brought from local farms and unloaded from boats to be transported by wagons drawn by horses, mules, or oxen to Cotton Row. (Courtesy Robert B. Williams, Photographic Collection, Hargrett Rare Book and Manuscript Library, University of Georgia Libraries.)

Richmond Academy. Augusta, Ga.

Shown here is the Academy of Richmond County, which was established in 1780. Both James U. Jackson and his father, George Twiggs Jackson, were students as were other family members. The school was on Telfair Street where the building can be seen today. (Courtesy Milledge G. Murray Collection.)

The Academy of Richmond County is pictured here as it appears today. The building is located on Telfair Street. (Courtesy Heritage Council of North Augusta.)

Lake Olmstead was created during the enlargement of the Augusta Canal between 1872 and 1875. The tunnels under the aqueduct were filled in, effectively damming Rae's Creek. (Courtesy Heritage Council of North Augusta.)

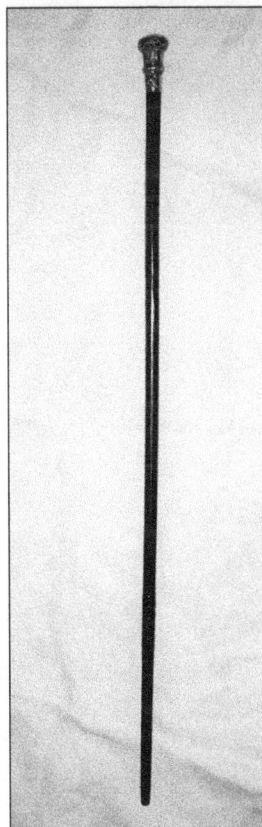

George T. Jackson was presented with this cane in 1875. He had served with the Confederate Army during the War Between the States. (Courtesy Hazel Jackson Boyles.)

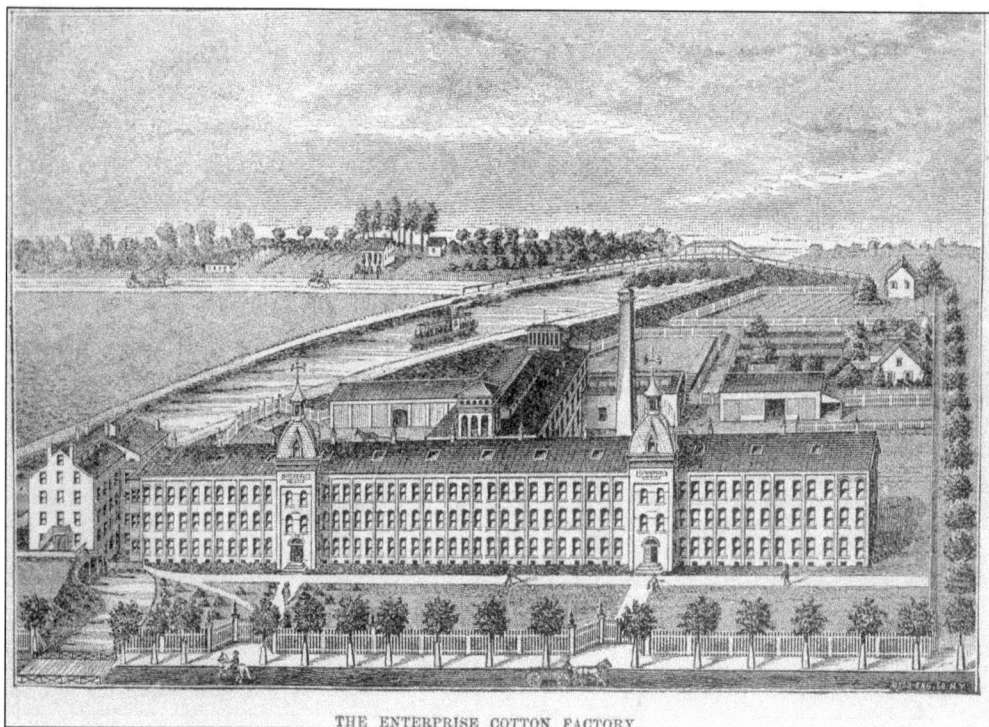

THE ENTERPRISE COTTON FACTORY.

In this etching of the Enterprise Mill, the Granite Mill owned by George T. Jackson can be seen at the left. (Courtesy Augusta Museum of History.)

Here is a recent photograph of the Enterprise Mill as it appears today. The building houses an interpretive center, the offices of the Augusta Canal Authority, and other businesses. Lofts, apartments, and condominiums make an attractive and interesting use of the space in the beautiful building. (Photograph Heritage Council of North Augusta. Courtesy Augusta Canal Authority.)

James P. Verdery took over the Enterprise Mill as president in 1886, and by 1888, it was profitable again. He remained president of the mill until 1917. (Courtesy Augusta Richmond County Historical Society, Reese Library, Augusta State University.)

University of Georgia.

DEAR SIR:

As an important part of the celebration of the Centennial of the University, the Board of Trustees has ordered the preparation and publication of a CENTENNIAL ALUMNI CATALOGUE, to contain, as far as possible, a full but concise account of the life and services of all the alumni during the century.

The hearty co-operation of all living alumni, and of the relatives and friends of all deceased, is necessary to the success of the undertaking. Your prompt and careful attention to the inquiries set forth below will be a real service to the University, and will be most cordially appreciated. If you are not able to give the information under any head, please leave the space *blank*, so that it may be filled by others.

The alma mater again extends to all alumni a hearty invitation to join with her in the celebration of the Centennial, June 12th—19th, 1901.

Fraternally yours,
WALTER B. HILL,
Chancellor.

1. Name, in full, (Do not use initials).

James Urquhart Jackson

2. Address; state, county, city, street and number:

Augusta Richmond Co Georgia

3. Place and time of birth:

June 24th 1856 Augusta Ga.

4. Date of entrance, with class entered:

Oct 1873 Sophomore Class

James U. Jackson completed this alumnus profile (this page and opposite) in 1901. He states that he entered the University of Georgia as a sophomore graduating in 1876 with a bachelor of science degree. He was a member of Phi Kappa and a published author of a work on securities of the South. Among relatives listed as alumni, James U. Jackson includes his brothers Walter and George Herbert, and his nephew, George T. Jackson. Under public service, he includes his role as director of the Augusta National Exposition Company. (Courtesy Hargrett Rare Book and Manuscript Library, University of Georgia Libraries.)

5. College honors, or distinctions of any kind:

Sophomore Declaimer
Graduated with Speakers place one of
two very distinguished
Graduated Capt of one of the Military Co
Senior Debater from Phi Kappa Society

6. Literary Society:

Phi Kappa

7. Date of graduation, and degree received, or date of leaving college:

August 1876. B. S

8. Other institutions attended later; degrees received; with dates:

9. Honorary degrees; by whom conferred, with dates:

10. Member of learned societies:

14. Writings.

Published & had copyrighted Book
on Securities of the South 1886

15. Any additional information of a personal nature:

Have been delegate from Augusta
to Several important Conventions
looking to the industrial development of the South

16. Names and addresses of any relatives, immediate or remote, who were
alumni:

Walter M. Jackson. G. Herbert
Jackson. Geo T Jackson all
Augusta Ga

11. Facts relating to marriage:

Married Nov 6th 1877 Minnie Talliaferro
at Athens Ga. Wife died Dec 1st 1885
Married second time Edith King
Mch 19th 1887 Savannah Ga
Had ten sons by first marriage one
now living. Had two sons & two daughters
by second marriage. All now living.

12. Facts as to occupation and business life:
Formed partnership with M J Verdery under
firm name of M J Verdery & Co 1876. Went
into business in myself 1884. Business that
of Security Broker. Negotiated many issues
of railroad Bonds & became Vice Pst
of M M & G R R 1886. Resigned 1889 ✱
Elected Vice Pst & Genl mngr Augusta
1893 resigned 1901. Now Genl Agent Seaboard Air Line R'y Co. One of reorganization
Committee Eagle & Phoenix Factory & Director two
years when resigned

13. Public service:
(a) Civil: Dates and titles of all public offices, appointments, or distinction:

Director Augusta National Exposition Co

(b) Military: Dates of service, name of commands, offices held:

Sergeant Sophyear Color Sergeant Battalion
Junior year. Captain Senior year.
Orderly Sergeant Richmond Troop

(c) Positions in religious or educational work, with dates:

35

Petersburg boats were once used to transport goods along the waterway. Today the Augusta Canal Authority conducts boat tours along the canal using reproductions of the Petersburg boats. (Photograph Heritage Council of North Augusta. Courtesy Augusta Canal Authority.)

OLD CONFEDERATE POWDER MILLS' CHIMNEY AND THE SIBLEY MILLS.

The Sibley Mill was built on the site of the Confederate Powder Works, which was demolished. The powder works chimney was saved and can be seen at left. Both the mill and the chimney remain relatively unchanged today. (Courtesy Augusta Museum of History.)

Furniture from the Jackson family home
in Harrisonville can be seen in these
photographs. The buffet (right) is part of
a dining set, which included a table and
several chairs that continues to be used
by the family. Both the dining set and
the cabinet are in the home of James U.
Jackson's grandson. (Courtesy George
Jackson Alexander.)

These two-story brick row houses can be seen along Broad Street. They were built for mill workers in the late 19th century. When mill workers were considering a strike in 1886, they were threatened with eviction from the mill housing and rethought their position. However, a few years later they did strike and were evicted. (Courtesy Heritage Council of North Augusta.)

King Mill is an impressive brick structure along the canal that continues to operate today as Standard Textiles. (Courtesy Heritage Council of North Augusta.)

George T. Jackson was a member of the building committee responsible for the construction of the library and Sunday School Building of the First Presbyterian Church. The building was demolished in 1976 as part of a new building program at the church. (Courtesy Augusta Museum of History.)

Minnie Falligant Jackson was James U. Jackson's first wife. She was 26 years old when she died in 1883. Her grave can be found in the Magnolia Cemetery in Augusta. The small grave on the right is that of James U. Jackson's first-born child. Robert Falligant Jackson was five months old when he died in 1880. (Courtesy Heritage Council of North Augusta.)

In this letter written by James U. Jackson in 1885 to Hon. W. N. Brawley of Charleston, South Carolina, Jackson makes reference to *Securities of the South*, a book copyrighted in 1886 entitled and mentioned in item 14 of his UGA alumnus profile. (Courtesy Milledge G. Murray Collection.)

Three Jackson brothers were on the baseball team of the Volunteer Fire Department No. 6. The brothers are pictured here in the back row; Charles Webster Jackson at the left, James U. Jackson is fourth from right, and the youngest brother, John, is second from right. John died in 1890, shortly after this photograph was taken. (Courtesy Augusta Richmond County Historical Society, Reese Library, Augusta State University.)

This photograph shows buildings under construction at the Exposition site the Augusta Exposition in 1888 attracted hundreds of visitors. Augusta's position at the head of navigation on the Savannah River and a railway system center attracted many northern business leaders. (Courtesy Augusta Museum of History.)

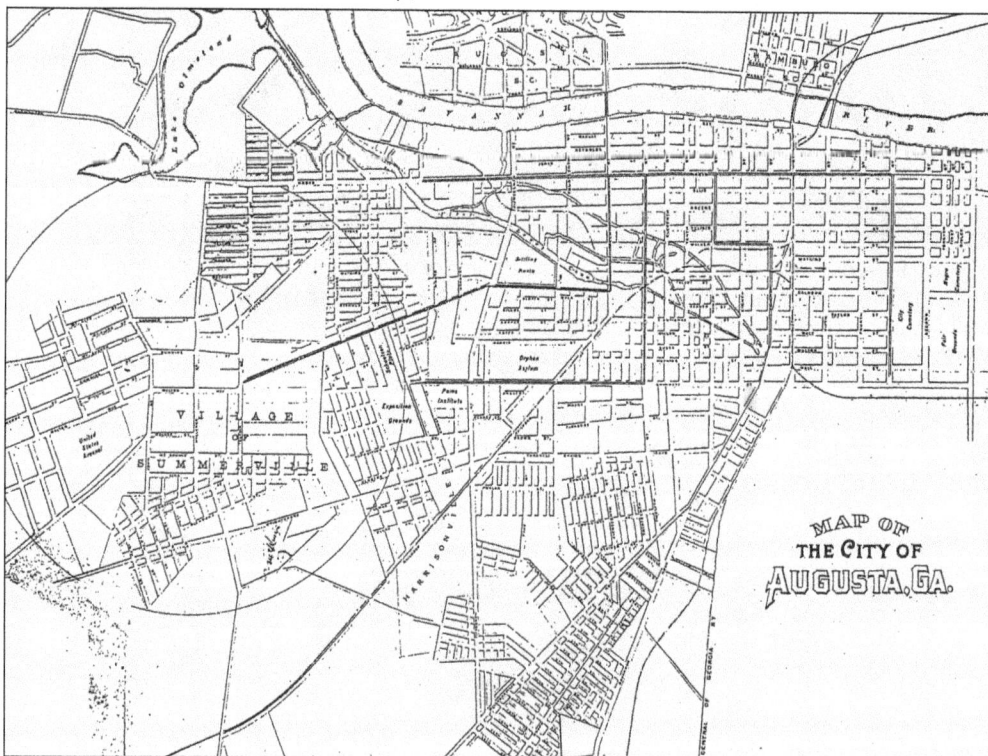

The location of the Exposition grounds is indicated on this map, which also identifies Harrisonville. (Courtesy Dr. Edward J. Cashin, Center for the Study of Georgia History, Augusta State University.)

Main Building of the Augusta Exposition.

The Augusta Exposition was held annually for several years. James U. Jackson was prominent
in its organization in 1888. This drawing is of the main exhibition building. (Courtesy Augusta
Richmond County Historical Society, Reese Library, Augusta State University.)

State of Georgia, Chatham County

Marriage License

BY HON. HAMPTON L. FERRILL

Ordinary for the County of Chatham and State aforesaid

To Any Minister of the Gospel, Jewish Minister, Judge, or Justice of the Peace of said State:

You are hereby authorized to join in the HOLY STATE OF MATRIMONY

Mr. James U. Jackson _____ of _____ Augusta, Ga.

Miss Edith B. King _____ and _____ of _____ Savannah, Ga.

according to the Constitution and Laws of the State, for which this shall be your License.

Given under my Hand and Seal of Office this ___ Eighteenth ___ day of

March ___ in the year of our Lord one thousand eight hundred and eighty nine.

Frank E. Keilbach

Clerk Court Ordinary Chatham County

James U. Jackson

This Certifies that ___

and Edith B. King ___ were duly Joined in Marriage

on the nineteenth ___ day of March ___ A.D. 1889

By me Charles F. Deems

Pastor, Church of the Strangers, New York

NOTE: RETURN TO ORDINARY FOR RECORD IMMEDIATELY AFTER CEREMONY.

James Urquhart Jackson and Edith Barrington King were married in Savannah in 1889. It was James Urquhart Jackson's second marriage. After the wedding, Jackson and his new bride lived at the family home in Harrisonville. (Courtesy George Jackson Alexander.)

Edith Barrington King was 24 years old when she married James U. Jackson in 1889; the groom was 33 years old. The wedding, which took place in Savannah, was a society event. The bride is pictured here in her wedding dress. (Courtesy George Jackson Alexander.)

James U. Jackson's sister, Leila, is pictured with family children outside the Jackson home in Harrisonville. It is not known when this photograph was taken. Leila moved back to Harrisonville as a widow in 1892. (Courtesy George Jackson Alexander.)

The Bon Air Hotel opened for the winter season in 1889. James U. Jackson was among the group of organizers who realized the potential for Augusta as a resort area. Noted industrialists, politicians, and presidents spent the winter season in Augusta, North Augusta, and Aiken to escape the harsher climate of the north. (Above courtesy Augusta Museum of History. Below courtesy Milledge G. Murray Collection.)

Bon Air Hotel, Summerville, near Augusta, Ga.

Three

REALIZING THE DREAM
1890–1906

In 1890, James U. Jackson formed the North Augusta Land Company. His father was living again with the family in Harrisonville. Retired from business, George T. Jackson listed his occupation as planter-farmer. George Twiggs Jackson would never again be seen in the arena in which for so many years he was such a powerful force. His son, however, comfortably filled that niche. Blessed with tireless energy, he was indefatigable. Various other family members were transitioning from the business of grocers into the business of railroads.

James U. Jackson, as a stock and bond broker and general manager of the North Augusta Land Company, purchased some 5,600 acres of North Augusta land from Mattie Butler Mealing for $100,000. The deed was signed on March 24, 1890. Jackson was a charismatic individual described on more than one occasion as having "a pleasing personality." He was an eloquent speaker possessed of charm. It was hard to overlook the intensity in his eyes and the sense of purpose and drive reflected there. Thus began the realization of a dream.

Critical to the development of North Augusta was providing access across the Savannah River. In May 1890, Jackson appeared before the mayor and city council in Augusta with his brother, Walter, and his cousin, William E., acting as attorney. They presented their petition with regards to the taxes levied on the new bridge project. One of the financial backers of the bridge was Marion Jackson Verdery of New York. The mayor and council decided in favor of the petitioners and freed the project from taxes. The annual meeting of the North Augusta Land Company was held February 2, 1891. Investors, either in person or by proxy, represented more than $80,000 of the $100,000 in capital stock of the company. William E. Jackson acted as secretary, and Marion Jackson Verdery and James U. Jackson were elected to the board. A local man seeking to purchase stock was informed that all the stock had been disposed of. A plan for the bridge was shown at the meeting, the New York investors looked over the property, and the financial arrangements were concluded. The steel bridge across the Savannah River connecting Augusta, Georgia, and North Augusta, South Carolina, was to be built at a cost of $85,000.

The scope and brilliance of the plan for the city of North Augusta was of utmost importance. The Charles Boeckh design of 1891 is applauded today, and James U. Jackson is praised more than 100 years later for his farsightedness in the plans. He was in New York for several weeks and returned at the end of September confident in having secured backing for his North Augusta project. Augusta felt confident in counting North Augusta as one of her most popular suburbs. Backers were enthusiastic to hear of the work already done in laying out boulevards and other developments. According to the *Augusta Chronicle*, the town felt in one year "it could look with considerable interest on the splendid heights across the river."

At the same time he was planning the city of North Augusta, Jackson was very much involved in planning railroads. Among the proposals was one to connect the Augusta and West Florida lines. The Richmond and Danville Railroad wished to complete a short line to Florida in competition with the Atlantic Coast Line. In June, the Augusta and West Florida Railroad trunk line was assured, and James U. Jackson was elected vice president. By August, the Carolina, Knoxville, and Western Railroad and the Augusta Railroad were virtually one system. James U. Jackson and William E. Jackson worked tirelessly to bring this about. The plan was to place Augusta in the middle of a valuable line from the mountains of Tennessee to the lakes of Florida.

James U. Jackson and his second wife, Edith, lived with their children and James U. Jackson's parents, just as he had with his first wife, Min. His older brother Walter, his wife, and their son; uncle John King's widow and sons William E. and John Hardwick; and other family members also lived at the family plantation in Harrisonville. Older sister Fanny, it must be assumed, always lived at the family home. Her sister, Leila, returned there as a widow in 1892. It would be so interesting if readers could identify the individuals pictured, although very small, around the home on Fifteenth Street in the image at the top of page 24.

In the fall of 1892, James U. Jackson was the second vice president of the annual carnival, King of Cotton. One could wonder if he might have worn his beaver-skin top hat.

During the years between 1892 and 1895, James U. Jackson's older brother Walter became the general manager of the North Augusta Land Company. James remained as a stock and bond broker with interests in railroads. He was elected president and general manager of the Augusta Southern Railroad in 1893. His cousins William E. and John Hardwick were attorneys, while brothers George Herbert and Charles Webster worked for the railroads. Cousin William E. Jackson Jr. was still with his widowed mother living and working on Greene Street.

James U. Jackson's older brother Walter built his home in North Augusta around 1895. Situated at the fork of Georgia and Carolina Avenues, Lookaway Hall is an impressive home in a perfect location. Both Lookaway Hall and Rosemary Hall were modeled after Barrington Hall in Roswell, Georgia, a home in Edith's family. Although very similar, the columns on all three are different. Lookaway's columns are in the Ionic style, and Rosemary's are in the Corinthian style. Originally plans called for both homes to be constructed on the lots where Lookaway Hall stands today. However, it was decided it would be too crowded. Legend has it that the site of each brother's home was decided on a cut of cards, with Walter the apparent winner. Willie Belle Munnerlyn, who was married to Walter's son, George T. Jackson, said many years later that her husband named the home Lookaway because of the view. After a hard day's work, he enjoyed sitting and relaxing on the wide front porch. Today Lookaway Hall still enjoys a beautiful view of Georgia Avenue toward the river.

George Jackson Verdery built his home about the same time Lookaway Hall was built. It can be seen today at the corner of West and Pine Grove Avenues. Resort hotels continued to be an important business now that rail travel made it easier for those living in the North to travel south for balmier weather during the winter months.

A streetcar system in Augusta had been in place for some time. Following the War Between the States, a streetcar pulled by mules covered the three miles from Summerville to Augusta on a plank road. Daniel Burns Dyer was responsible for bringing electric power to Augusta. It was he who "lit up" Broad Street in 1892.

In 1897, James U. Jackson brought the trolley to North Augusta. It facilitated movement between Augusta and North Augusta's Natatorium, a favorite recreational area. Initially the line ran to Crystal Lake; it was later extended to Jackson Avenue.

Luther Arrington, who became North Augusta's first mayor, built a beautiful home at the corner of Jackson and Georgia Avenues. The home and several others were razed over the years, as "progress" sometimes dictates.

One can still see the Benson family home. Originally it stood on Georgia Avenue and was moved to the rear of the lot when the Exxon station was built. In 1999, it was moved again to its present location on West Avenue where it is home to the Family Physicians of North Augusta. Berry Benson served throughout the War Between the States as a sharpshooter and a scout. He was imprisoned at Elmira but managed to escape. Benson never surrendered his rifle and returned to North Augusta after the war. He worked for many years as an accountant in Augusta. A statue of Berry Benson can be seen today atop a column on Broad Street in Augusta, standing above four generals. He is buried in North Augusta's Sunset Hill Cemetery.

James U. Jackson was unanimously re-elected president of the Augusta Southern Railroad at the annual meeting of stockholders in April 1897. He left Augusta for Columbus in June to attend a meeting of the reorganization committee of the Eagle and Phoenix Manufacturing Company. The energy and drive of Jackson were amazing!

A meeting of the North Augusta community was held in 1898 to discuss education. The community raised $300, and a schoolhouse was built on the east side of West Avenue between Pine Grove and Buena Vista Avenues, on a lot donated by the North Augusta Land Company. Nina Verdery, the teacher, had 13 students. Today the schoolhouse is an antique shop. The Heritage Council of North Augusta, to acknowledge the schoolhouse's part in North Augusta's history, placed a historic marker on the building in 2001.

James U. Jackson found himself in court in August 1898 as temporary receiver and president of the Augusta Southern Railroad in a battle between the Augusta Southern and the South Carolina and Georgia Railroad. Augusta Southern was the petitioner for permanent receivership pending a suit to break the lease by the South Carolina and Georgia. Most of the affidavits dealt with dissatisfactions of shipments (cotton) by the Augusta Southern while the South Carolina and Georgia had controlled it. It was alleged good engines and coaches of the Augusta Southern Railroad were put on the South Carolina and Georgia while the Augusta Southern was compelled to use inferior rolling stock. James U. Jackson's brother, Charles Webster, was the railroad's freight agent. The following year, he worked as a passenger and freight agent at Augusta Southern. The petition charged the South Carolina and Georgia Railroad had conspired to injure the plaintiff's property for the purpose of forcing a sale and to enable the defendant (South Carolina and Georgia Railroad) to obtain absolute control. Jackson stated the railroad had a loss of $21,000 where previously there had been a profit of $27,000 for a corresponding period. His brother, Charles Webster, as division freight agent made a statement regarding secret rate cutting, particularly of cotton bound for the Charleston area over local cotton destined for Augusta. In September, the judge ordered Jackson of the Augusta Southern and Joseph H. Sands of the South Carolina and Georgia be appointed as coreceivers.

James U. Jackson's father, George Twiggs Jackson, died at his home in Harrisonville on February 4, 1899. After an illness of several months, George T. died surrounded by his wife and family. A brilliant businessman and patriarch of the Jackson family, he had made an impact on the city of Augusta. Apart from his mill, banking, and railroad interests, he was one of the original subscribers to the Augusta Orphan Asylum. Both he and his brother, William E., were trustees. George T. was a member of the building committee of the orphan asylum. Today the Tuttle-Newton Home is located on Central Avenue. Members of the board serve for life, as they did more than 100 years ago. As a soldier, George T. Jackson had responded to General Beauregard's call for volunteers when Charleston was threatened with bombardment from ironclads, and he had been promoted to commander of the Augusta Battalion.

At the end of the year, a commission of prominent citizens proposed to take steps to persuade

President McKinley to visit Augusta. James U. Jackson guaranteed special rates on his Augusta Southern Railroad to attract people for such a visit. In 1899, President McKinley visited Camp McKenzie, a tent city near Wheeless Station on the Georgia Railroad, and he was persuaded by Mayor Patrick Walsh to make a short speech at the Confederate monument.

James U. Jackson met with president John Skelton Williams and others of Seaboard Air Line Railroad when they came to Augusta at the end of 1899. As general agent of the system, he served as the master of ceremonies. The Harrison block across from the Augusta depot had been purchased for the purpose of turning it over to Seaboard if they decided to build into Augusta. Seaboard was expected to bring substantial passenger and freight business to the city.

John Cranston built his beautiful home on the hill on Carolina Avenue in 1900. As a business associate of James U. Jackson, the Cranston and Jackson families socialized on many occasions. Unfortunately the home is one of those lost to progress over the years. A home that has been saved is the Fearey home on Georgia Avenue, which now houses the Greater North Augusta Chamber of Commerce.

Although he had been a staunch Democrat and supported the policies and principles of that party, Jackson declared himself in support of McKinley, the Republican incumbent. Having read the platforms of both McKinley and Democrat William Jennings Bryan, he felt McKinley would be of more benefit to the entire country, especially the South. He stated, "I believe our railroads and manufacturing and all other industries and enterprises will be more benefited by the re-election of McKinley."

Far removed from national-level politics, elections were held in 1901 in the village of Harrisonville. Of the eight contestants, five were elected, including George Herbert. William E. and James U. Jackson were unsuccessful. Jackson resigned as president of the Augusta Southern Railroad due to duties with Seaboard Air Line Railroad. In turn, the Augusta Southern Railroad was sold to the Southern Railway. Jackson began planning to build a water plant in North Augusta and a family home for Edith and him and their four children. Contracts were awarded in May for both projects. John Skelton Williams, president of the Seaboard Air Line Railroad, and J. W. Middendorf (sometimes spelled Mittendorff), financial agent of the company, were close business associates and backers of Jackson over many years. John Skelton Williams was a former comptroller of U.S. currency and a partner in Williams and Middendorf of New York. James U. Jackson represented the railway as general agent during 1901. He worked to secure an extension of Southern Railway's rights regarding the Greater Seaboard System and the Chattanooga, Augusta, and Charleston Air Line Railway as part of that system. It was one of the many business enterprises in which James U. Jackson worked tirelessly. Also in May 1901, Jackson announced the future construction of the Augusta-Aiken Electric Road. Returning from a trip to New York, Baltimore, Richmond, and Philadelphia, he announced the first five miles of the road would be in operation by August. The International Trust Company of Maryland in Baltimore was the trustee for the bonds; everything for the construction had been purchased, including cars, rails, wire, and cross ties. Surveying crews were already at work. Jackson became president of the North Augusta Electric and Improvement Company in 1902 and moved his offices from the Dyer Building on Broad Street in August of that year.

He then purchased the Augusta Railway and Electric Company from D. B. Dyer, and thus began the first interurban road in the South. It was powered by electricity generated at a steam plant on the Clearwater Road. The Augusta-Aiken Railway linked Aiken, North Augusta, and Augusta, facilitating travel between the great resort hotels in Aiken and Augusta. James U. Jackson Jr. turned the first shovel of dirt for the interurban road, which operated for almost 30 years. Passengers could make the journey from the Bon Air Hotel in Augusta to Aiken via North Augusta, a distance of about 20 miles, for a fare of 50¢ round trip. One car was a combination passenger/baggage. Freight cars were used to transport goods.

Jackson built his home on the corner of Forest and Carolina Avenues in 1902. He hand-selected most of the materials himself, including the rosemary pine. The family home would not be referred to as Rosemary Hall until 1915. With 22 rooms and a porch supported by

50-foot Corinthian columns, it is a gracious home. The beautiful English staircase is one of its outstanding features. Home to Jackson, Edith, and their four children, the house was the scene of many parties, dinners, and the weddings of daughters Daisy and Edith. As part of the application process to the National Register of Historic places in 1974, Edith Alexander, James U. Jackson's daughter, who was an accomplished artist, made several sketches of the home's features.

In April 1902, John Williams Jackson, James U. Jackson's youngest child, named for Seaboard Air Line president John Skelton Williams, turned the first shovel of dirt for the proposed Hampton Terrace resort hotel, named for Gen. Wade Hampton. Preliminary construction was underway for Jackson's next enterprise.

The Woodward Lumber Company was awarded the construction contract, and work began on the Hampton Terrace Hotel. There were rumors of friction between Walter M. Jackson and the contractors, but they were put to rest by Walter, who stated that 500 mechanics and laborers were working on the project and it was progressing satisfactorily, adding that it would be ready for guests by January 1, 1903. The interurban railway was used to carry many materials, including in May 1902, when 35 carloads of plasterboard to be used in the construction of a fireproof interior were transported. The Hampton Terrace Hotel on the hill in North Augusta was planned to have accommodations for 500 guests with 300 rooms. In the Gilded Age, privileged guests traveled with furniture and servants for a stay of two or three months. Redwood double doors separated all the *en suite* rooms, and brick surrounded each elevator well. There was a music room and sun parlors where guests could retire after dinner to play cards—four-handed euchre was popular at the time. There were amusements to suit every taste: dancing, billiards, tennis, shuffleboard, and ping-pong. In front of the hotel was a carefully laid-out golf course with nine holes ready for the opening season and a further nine holes to be completed by the following winter. A circular driveway, made by cutting and terracing, aided a gradual approach to the hotel. There was excellent fishing and access to a 15,000-acre game preserve owned by Jackson. The Hampton Terrace Hotel was an enormous success both commercially and personally for Jackson. Guests included the most influential people of the time. John D. Rockefeller, Marshall Field, and Harvey Firestone leased entire wings and floors of the grand hotel. Marshall Field's sons stayed at the Jacksons' home during their family's visits. For more than a dozen years, it was one of the premier winter resorts, until the tragic events of December 31, 1916, when the hotel was totally destroyed by fire.

Businesses were developing in the North Augusta riverfront area. Mark Baynham began a pottery business around 1900 in the bottomland close to the river. T. L. Horne established a pottery business in 1903 at West and Bluff Avenues. There were two brick companies, an abattoir, and a coal company. In 1904, the Industrial Lumber Company was among the early businesses in a flourishing North Augusta. There was a blacksmith, and by 1912, a box factory and chair factory were located in the riverfront area.

The North Augusta Dispensary was established in 1907. The Aiken City Board of Control determined that due to the fact Georgia was "dry," establishing a dispensary just across the river was good business. They acquired the office building of the Hankinson Brick Company in the old Shapira building. A spur track of the Southern Railroad was located there, and the interurban railway also made a stop. Prohibition brought about the demise of the dispensary. Along with businesses, homes also continued to be built in the prospering town of North Augusta.

In May 1903, attorneys Verdery and Jackson requested a charter for North Augusta. Later that summer, an article in the *Baltimore Sun* in August reported James U. Jackson, general agent of the Seaboard Air Line Railroad, was in town for an Elks convention. Jackson was a member of Augusta Lodge 205, whose badge bore a reproduction of the famous Elberta peach. The lodge brought 60 crates of the peaches, raised near their home, to be tossed to spectators along the parade route. Jackson spoke earnestly of the economy, saying "farmers are in better shape than before the war." Money was plentiful and cotton prices high. "We are no longer dependent on cotton alone, early vegetables, berries, melons, and peaches bring prompt returns."

Since 1890, there had been talk of selling the Augusta Canal. In August 1903, Jackson raised the issue again, "I think to sell the canal is the best thing to do and I should like to see it done. In a few months new factories would begin to rise on the canal adding wealth and population to the city." He felt the city would benefit financially, but opponents were just as strong in their beliefs. In September, discussions began on the establishment of a racetrack in North Augusta. Jackson invited a committee of prominent Augustans to view the land for the proposed track.

September 1903 was also the month discussions began on the establishment of a new county with North Augusta as the county seat. Aiken and Edgefield counties were so large and the county seats situated in such a manner it required a 20- to 25-mile journey to conduct business. This could mean a day's work lost on one's farm or business to make a trip to the county seat. The boundaries of the proposed new county would be, very roughly, from the Savannah River to Modoc, Clarks Hill, and Colliers, on to Langley, Beech Island, and Sleepy Hollow. A committee was appointed, as many arrangements had to be made before an election could be called by the governor of South Carolina. A second committee was named to solicit funds and survey the limits of the proposed new county. Jackson agreed to finance the survey so that it might begin at once. There was considerable discord in the December election, and the move for a new county was defeated. The community of Bath voted heavily against the proposal. By 8 p.m., the vote was 394 against the new county and 204 for the new county, and even with remaining precincts to be counted, the outcome could not change.

Also in 1903, James U. Jackson sold a lot for $1.00 so that Grace Methodist Episcopal Church South, which became United Methodist Church, might build in North Augusta. Today it is known as Grace United Methodist Church. He gave the address and deposited articles in the cornerstone in July 1903. Edith, James, and daughters Edith and Daisy became members in 1905. The following year he gave a lot to be used for a parsonage. It was deeded over in 1912.

The Hampton Terrace Hotel continued to be a favorite destination for the privileged of the Gilded Age. The trolley ran north on West Avenue, where the smokestack of the hotel could be seen in the distance. Very little remains today of the great hotel, but one can see the brick remains of the smokestack on Butler Avenue across from Fairview Presbyterian Church.

In North Augusta, businesses continued to prosper. Hollis Boardman founded People's Oil Company. He established a plant under the Thirteenth Street Bridge. Boardman had been employed by John D. Rockefeller's Standard Oil Company. With People's, he began one of the first independent oil companies in the South. The many cotton mills in Augusta and the Horse Creek Valley were its principal customers.

A telegraph order system was established on the trolley line at the Natatorium and the Hampton Terrace Hotel station. A system of colored signal lamps had previously been used. Arrangements were made for the trolley conductor to handle mail pouches. There were two daily mails, with three in the tourist season. Mrs. Frey kept the first post office in North Augusta in the hall of her home. By 1904, the post office was located in a store near the corner of Pine Grove and Georgia Avenues.

Jackson entertained Frank Harris, the treasurer of Pennsylvania, and the presidents of several banks at the Hampton Terrace Hotel. They went hunting at Yemassee and toured the Jackson properties. Cumbahee Hunting Club owned 6,000 to 10,000 acres in fee and had exclusive privileges to an adjoining 15,000 acres for hunting partridge, deer, turkey, ducks, and foxes. The old hotel at Yemassee had been converted to a clubhouse where every convenience and comfort was provided.

On December 5, 1904, Catherine Jackson, James U. Jackson's mother, died at her home in Harrisonville. Of her children, Leila, Fanny, and George Herbert were with her. James was in New York on business, and Walter was in Athens, Georgia, for a funeral. Although she had been ill for some time, her death was unexpected. Nephews George J., Albert M., L. F. Verdery, William E., John Hardwick, and William E. Jackson Jr. acted as pallbearers.

Two other properties of interest were built around this time. The first was Palmetto Lodge. Originally built as a lodge for the Hampton Terrace Hotel, it became a private residence when purchased by New Yorkers and winter visitors the John Herberts. They named it Palmetto Lodge. Located in the Georgia Avenue/Butler Avenue Historic District, it has been occupied by several families over the years, most notably the writer Edison Marshall. It has been said that while spending time at Palmetto Lodge, Harvey Firestone became engaged to a local girl; apparently the relationship ended.

Another interesting property is at the corner of Carolina Avenue and Arlington Heights. A private residence for many years, at the time the Hampton Terrace Hotel flourished it was a tearoom operated by Mrs. Emery Platt Ruland. The family lived in a home on Carolina Avenue adjacent to the tearoom. After the disastrous fire at the Hampton Terrace Hotel, those who continued to play golf on the hotel course used the building for several years.

In 1904, James U. Jackson instituted a plan for the reorganization of all the companies under a single company owned and controlled by one large financial institution. A company was formed in Trenton, New Jersey, with unlimited capital. At the meeting of the board of directors, James U. Jackson was elected president of each division, including the North Augusta Land Company, the North Augusta Electric and Improvement Company, the Augusta-Aiken Railway Company, and the Augusta Railway and Electric Company. The Honorable Boykin Wright had been counsel for the latter and would continue in that role. The other companies being incorporated in South Carolina would be represented by Henry Buist of Charleston.

The North Augusta Tennis Club was formed in the summer of 1905 with meetings to be held at the Hampton Terrace Hotel. Members of the Augusta Railway and Electric Company Benefit Association were dissatisfied and explored the possibility of joining the national union but determined it would be in their best interests to remain with the local group.

Even at the pace of the 21st century, the energy and drive of Jim Jackson is staggering. He was a master of multi-tasking long before the term was coined. The number of projects undertaken, to say nothing of the responsibilities as president of several companies, he was astonishing. James and Edith entertained lavishly with teas, receptions, and oyster suppers all being held at the family home with guest lists of 12 to 20 or more.

In early 1906, he returned from New York with a new project, a railroad from Augusta to Valdosta. Frequent business ally John Skelton Williams would head the enterprise. The opportunity was prompted by a recent sale of the Augusta Florida, which operated 47 miles of track on the Augusta Southern from Keysville to Swainsboro.

Meetings were held every evening on the matter of incorporation. Of the 93 registered voters, 85 went to the polls; the vote was 56 to 29 in favor of incorporation. The state of South Carolina issued a charter, and North Augusta became a corporate municipality on April 11, 1906. The charter was revised in 1912. The population by 1913 was 1,500. The town at that time had a water and sewerage plant, schools, and a public library.

The movement to form a new county began again, with North Augusta as its county seat. It must be noted that under the laws of the state of South Carolina no new county could be formed without an incorporated village. There continued to be heavy opposition to the proposal. A banquet held at the Hampton Terrace Hotel discussed the proposed new county, and a meeting was held to set the laws of the new municipality. The matter of police and fire departments was addressed, and a number of improvements were planned. In October 1906, it was reported that Jackson and nephew, George T. Jackson, associate counsel for the railway, would present and argue the case for Heyward County (the name for the proposed new county) before South Carolina governor Duncan Clinch Heyward. Both men were positive about the outcome and ready to set a date for the election. The matter of a new county with North Augusta as its county seat would be raised again and again over the next several years.

Jackson was temporary chairman of the Georgia-Carolina Fair Association—with all his many responsibilities and business interests, it's difficult to believe he could be interested in yet another venture. Nevertheless he made a generous offer on the Monte Sano Park property in Augusta. It was the site of a summer theater that had burned the previous year. The plans were to build a new tourist hotel on the high ground of the site with open country behind.

The street railway ran in front of the property, making for a very convenient trip to the city. Meanwhile surveyors were working near Batesburg on another proposed Jackson project, a line from Columbia to Augusta through Aiken. No property had been purchased for the right of way, but it was not expected the property-owning farmers affected would be adverse to such a project.

In September 1906, James U. Jackson went to New York to personally present William Jennings Bryan with an invitation to visit Augusta during the Fall Fair. Marion Jackson Verdery was among the party received "with most perfect courtesy and hospitality." Bryan did not set a definite date for his visit, but it was expected he would attend.

The fair was to be held October 29 through November 3, 1906. It is known that Bryan visited Augusta on a campaigns swing and dined with local dignitaries at the Albion Hotel in September on his way to Atlanta. It is not known for certain if he returned for the Fall Fair.

The North Augusta Land Company was formed in 1890. James U. Jackson is pictured fourth from the left in the front row. Unfortunately the other individuals are unidentified. (Courtesy North Augusta Historical Society.)

GEORGE T. JACKSON, JR.,
ATTORNEY AT LAW,
325-326 DYER BUILDING.

In Re: "Old Cross Tract."   Augusta, Ga. July 25, 1899

Mr. Henry A. M. Smith
No. 31 Broad St. Charleston, S.C.

Dear Sir;

Your favor of the 24th inst. just to hand, and your proposition therein contained in regard to the settlement of Mrs. Middleton's claim for dower is entirely satisfactory, and if you will kindly advise me as to what Savings Bank in Charleston you would desire the money deposited in, I will send rough draft of bond and mortgage for your inspection, and I will be glad to have you make any corrections or suggestions you may think advisable, as you say you have upon several occasions arranged similar matters. Upon second thought, — I herewith enclose draft of bond and mortgage, leaving blanks for you to fill in and return and we will execute it in due form. The deed from your clients to us is to be made to James U. Jackson.

Very truly yours Geo T. Jackson.

This is a letter written by attorney George T. Jackson, James U. Jackson's nephew and son of Jackson's older brother, Walter. Written on letterhead from an office in the Dyer Building. The Jacksons moved their offices from the building when James U. Jackson purchased the Augusta Railway and Electric Company from Daniel Burns Dyer in 1902. (Courtesy Milledge G. Murray Collection.)

In Augusta and North Augusta at the end of the 19th century, most local transportation was by a wagon and team, horse and buggy, or oxcart. James U. Jackson, following the lead of D. B. Dyer, was about to change that. (Courtesy North Augusta Historical Society.)

The North Augusta Bridge was built in 1891 at a cost of $85,000. It facilitated travel between Augusta and its new suburb, North Augusta. (Above courtesy Augusta Museum of History. Below courtesy Special Collections, Reese Library, Augusta State University.)

These are the signatures of the individuals who, in two carriages, crossed the new bridge in October 1891. Taking part in the bridge-opening ceremony were James U. Jackson, his brothers Walter and George Herbert, and nephews George T. and William E., as well as local dignitaries. (Courtesy George Jackson Alexander.)

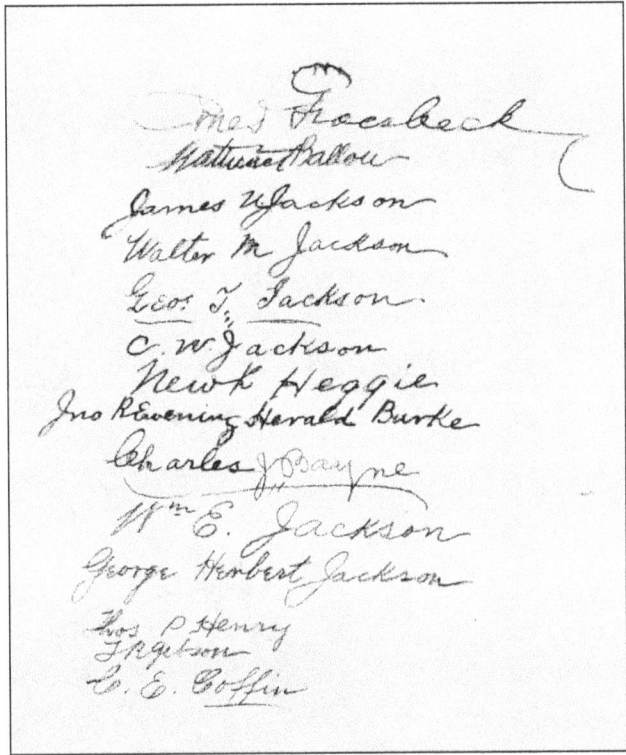

Lookaway Hall was built around 1895 behind Calhoun Park at the junction of Georgia and Carolina Avenues. The house, built for James U. Jackson's brother Walter, was given the name Lookaway by Walter's son, George T. Jackson. Lookaway has become a symbol of North Augusta. (Photograph Heritage Council of North Augusta. Courtesy Sandra L. Croy.)

The Charles Boeckh Plan of 1891 is applauded today for its farsightedness. A civil engineer from Delaware, the plan included small parks and open spaces following swales toward the Savannah River. Today it might be construed as wetlands preservation. (Courtesy City of North Augusta.)

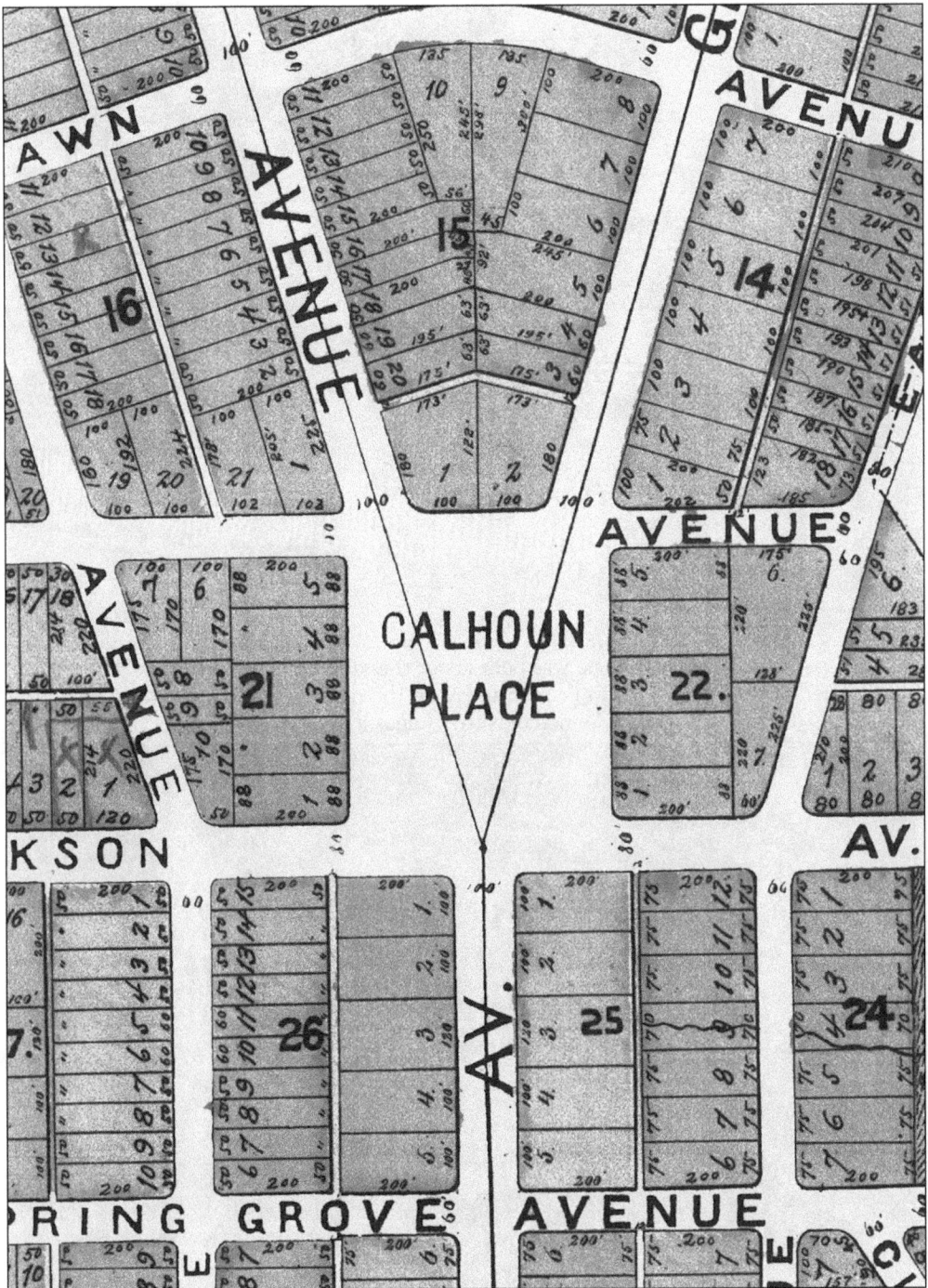

The area behind Calhoun Park where Lookaway Hall stands was originally platted for both James U. Jackson and his brother Walter to construct their homes, one facing Carolina Avenue, the other Georgia Avenue. However, the brothers decided this arrangement would be too crowded. (Courtesy City of North Augusta.)

The George Jackson Verdery Home was built about the same time as Lookaway Hall. Sold in 1919 to the Buckner family, it can be seen today on the northwest corner of West Avenue at Pine Grove. (Courtesy Heritage Council of North Augusta.)

This early photograph of the North Augusta Bridge shows a trolley passing a horse-drawn vehicle. (Courtesy Charles E. Petty.)

The Natatorium was a popular recreational area. Many Augustans rode the streetcar to North Augusta to go swimming. The Natatorium was located in the area of present-day Crystal Lake. (Courtesy North Augusta Historical Society.)

This was the home of North Augusta's first mayor. Luther Arrington served from April 16, 1906, to September 6, 1906. Initially North Augusta's mayors served one-year terms. Arrington's wife died an a fire, but the date of that incident is not known. It may have been the reason he decided to move back to property he owned on Broad Street and resign after six months. The Bates family lived in the home for many years and, in turn, sold it to Kate Kirkland. She sold the house in 1938 so that the site might be used for a North Augusta high school. (Courtesy North Augusta Historical Society.)

The Foreman home was located at the corner of Buena Vista and West Avenues, where Wetherington Builders has their office today. The Foreman family operated several businesses in North Augusta over the years. (Courtesy Charles E. Petty.)

Wachovia Bank, at the corner of Georgia and Buena Vista Avenues, occupies the site of the Frey Home, which was razed so that a bank might be built. (Courtesy North Augusta Historical Society.)

The Murphy home was located at the corner of Jackson and West Avenues. The beloved Sno Cap Drive-In, which occupies the site today, was built in 1964. (Courtesy North Augusta Historical Society.)

This was probably the Turner home, located on the corner of West and Buena Vista Avenues. New buildings in the area have been constructed with designs that compliment existing properties and the surrounding area. (Courtesy Charles E. Petty.)

The Benson Home was originally built for another family and was located on Georgia Avenue where Carpenter's Exxon Station stands today. The house was relocated to a site behind the station and in 1999 moved to its present location on West Avenue. (Courtesy North Augusta Historical Society.)

The Berry Benson home today houses the Family Physicians of North Augusta. (Courtesy Heritage Council of North Augusta.)

Berry Benson was born in Hamburg, South Carolina. According to legend, his boots were never tied. He served as a scout and sharpshooter during the War Between the States. Benson served throughout the conflict and was imprisoned, but he escaped. At the end of the war, he returned to North Augusta, never having surrendered his rifle. That rifle can be seen today at the Augusta Museum of History. (Courtesy Charles E. Petty.)

The first schoolhouse in North Augusta was constructed in 1898 on land donated by James U. Jackson and the North Augusta Land Company. Today it is home to Singing Hills Antiques and can be seen on West Avenue between Pine Grove and Buena Vista Avenues. (Courtesy Heritage Council of North Augusta.)

Nina Verdery, North Augusta's first schoolteacher, was one of George Jackson Verdery's five daughters. (Courtesy North Augusta Historical Society.)

George Twiggs Jackson, James U. Jackson's father, died in 1899 and is buried in Augusta's Magnolia Cemetery. (Courtesy Heritage Council of North Augusta.)

George T. Jackson was one of the original subscribers to the Augusta Orphan Asylum. He was a member of the building committee in 1871. The building was ready for occupation at the end of 1873. Destroyed by fire in 1889, it was rebuilt by the end of 1890. Originally on a site bounded by Harper Street and South Boundary and the Georgia Railroad, the facility has been relocated more than once. It was decided at a meeting held in 1915 to rename the institution in honor of Mr. Tuttle and Dr. Newton. The word asylum would be dropped. The name change did not occur officially until 1919. Today the Tuttle-Newton Home is on Central Avenue. (Courtesy Tuttle-Newton Home.)

Augusta's Union Station was located at Ninth and Walker Streets. This photograph shows the station around 1890. James U. Jackson was instrumental in securing the Union Station for Augusta. (Courtesy Augusta Museum of History.)

The beautiful Cranston home was on the top of the hill on Carolina Avenue. In 1972, the home was razed, and the Holy Lutheran Church was constructed on the site. (Courtesy Milledge G. Murray Collection.)

Originally, this was home of local businessman James Fearey, located on Clifton Avenue behind Wade Hampton Veterans Park; Today it is home today to the Greater North Augusta Chamber of Commerce. (Courtesy Heritage Council of North Augusta.)

Dyer Building, Augusta, Ga.

The Dyer Building on Broad Street was Augusta's first office building. James U. Jackson and his nephew, George T. Jackson, had offices there. Sun Trust Bank occupies the site today. (Courtesy Milledge G. Murray Collection.)

THE DYER BLOCK.

This view of the Dyer Building shows a trolley on Broad Street. Daniel Burns Dyer was the owner of the Augusta Railway and Electric Company. James U. Jackson bought the company from him, and by 1902, the company ran an interurban road linking Augusta, North Augusta, and Aiken. (Courtesy Special Collections, Reese Library, Augusta State University.)

James U. Jackson Jr. was about six years old when he turned the first shovel of dirt for the construction of the interurban road. (Courtesy *The Augusta Chronicle*.)

One of the cars used on the interurban road is pictured here. The wooden cars were painted red and had about 50 seats; some cars had curtains at the windows. (Courtesy North Augusta Historical Society.)

TROLLEY

TRANSPORTATION

IS

SAFEST

MOST DEPENDABLE

CHEAPEST

HYDRO POWER

IN ANY QUANTITY

FOR EVERY PURPOSE.

RELIABLE SERVICE

REASONABLE RATES

**Augusta - Aiken
Railway & Electric Corporation**

This advertisement for the trolley line describes the safety and dependability of the new interurban road. The trolley line contributed to the development of North Augusta. Its small stations became places where passengers might socialize while waiting, sometimes pausing for tea in a tea room. (Courtesy North Augusta Historical Society.)

This photograph shows freight cars of the interurban road being loaded. Local goods, including cotton, vegetables, fruits, and building materials were transported. The interurban road was a major handler of freight for the area. (Courtesy Charles E. Petty.)

Rosemary Hall, home of North Augusta's founder, James U. Jackson, is on Carolina Avenue at the northwest corner of Forest Avenue. (Photograph Heritage Council of North Augusta. Courtesy Sandra L. Croy.)

This is Rosemary Hall's beautiful English staircase. The first flight rises from the entry and divides to provide access to the second-floor rooms. The staircase is original to the home, which was built in 1902. Perhaps only the author was reminded of a scene from *Gone With the Wind* on seeing it for the first time. (Photograph Heritage Council of North Augusta. Courtesy Sandra L. Croy.)

Shown here is the dining room of Rosemary Hall today. James U. Jackson and his wife entertained a great deal; a number people of note in the Gilded Age would have enjoyed a meal at this table. (Photograph Heritage Council of North Augusta. Courtesy Sandra L. Croy.)

This is the ladies' parlor of the home; the gentlemen's parlor is across the hall. At the time when Edith and James U. Jackson entertain guests, the ladies probably retired to this parlor, while the gentleman enjoyed cigars and brandy in the dining room. (Photograph Heritage Council of North Augusta. Courtesy Sandra L. Croy.)

Shown here is one of several bedrooms in Rosemary Hall. Today the home is a bed and breakfast Inn catering to the comfort of its guests. A recent guest in this particular room was Lance Armstrong while in Augusta for the Tour de Georgia. (Photograph Heritage Council of North Augusta. Courtesy Sandra L. Croy.)

This is the beautiful pine-paneled landing on the second floor. Built by local artisans, James U. Jackson personally selected the materials used. (Photograph Heritage Council of North Augusta. Courtesy Sandra L. Croy.)

Side windows to front door.
E.B.J. Alexander
1974

This is a sketch of a window by the front door. These windows flank the entrance to the home and are original to the house. James U. Jackson's daughter, Edith Barrington Alexander, an accomplished artist, made these sketches in 1974. They were part of the application process for Rosemary hall to be included in the National Register of Historic Places.

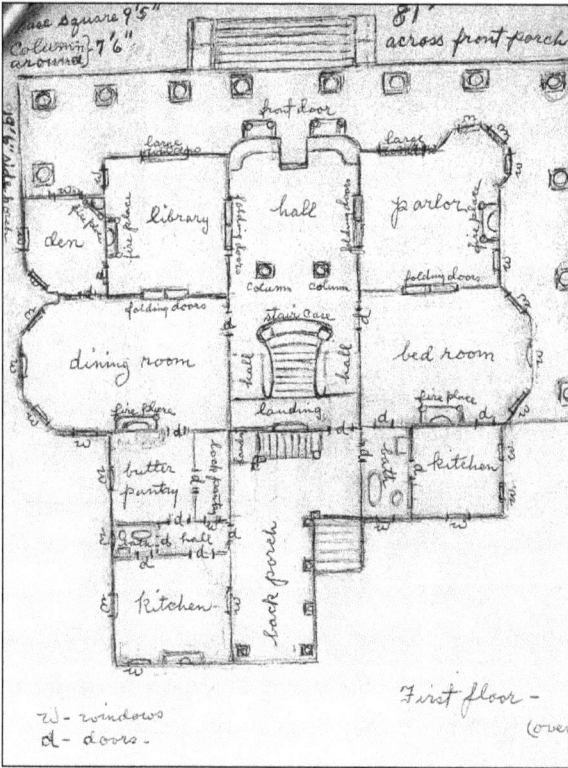

Sketched here is a plan of the first floor by Edith Barrington Alexander.

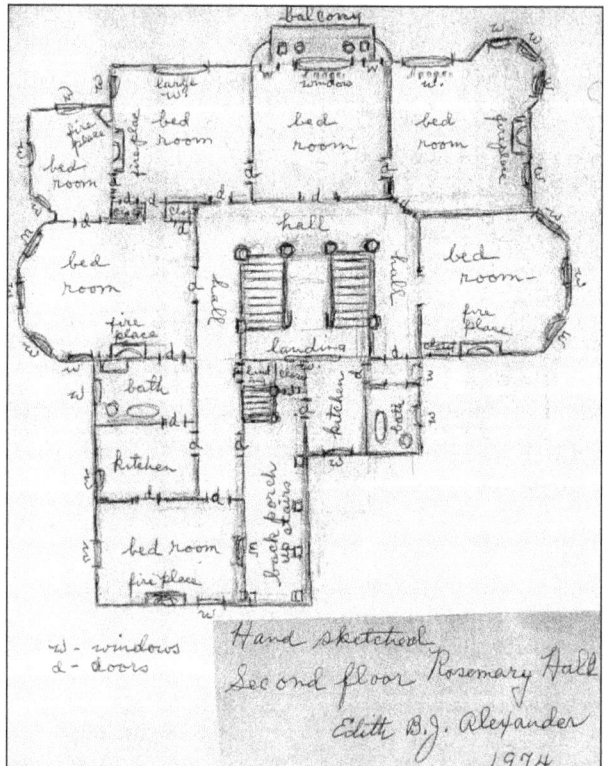

This is a plan of the second floor. James U. Jackson's daughter, Edith, did these sketches as part of the application process to the National Register of Historic Places. (Courtesy National Register of Historic Places, South Carolina Department of Archives and History.)

Built at a cost of more than half a million dollars, the Hampton Terrace Hotel consisted of five floors, four of which had accommodations for 500 guests in 300 rooms. (Courtesy North Augusta Historical Society.)

Many potted palms decorated the lobby of the Hampton Terrace Hotel. Typical of the decorating style of the Gilded Age, Oriental carpets covered the polished floors. (Courtesy North Augusta Historical Society.)

This photograph is of the Rotunda at the Hampton Terrace Hotel. It had a glass ceiling and was open on three floors with seating arranged for guests to enjoy the music drifting up from the rotunda floor. One can see such an open area with seats at the top of this postcard. (Courtesy Joseph M. Lee III.)

Shown here is the number-one green of the Hampton Terrace golf course. The fairways stretched from Arlington Heights across East Avenue toward present day North Augusta Plaza and the Community Center. (Courtesy Joseph M. Lee III.)

The Industrial Lumber Company was an early North Augusta business. It supplied local businesses in both Augusta and North Augusta with materials. (Courtesy Charles E. Petty.)

The North Augusta Dispensary was built close to the North Augusta Bridge in 1907 to take advantage of business in Georgia, which was dry. Prohibition brought about the dispensary's demise. (Courtesy Charles E. Petty.)

This grocery store was an early North Augusta business located near the dispensary. Those pictured were probably the owner and employees of the store. From the sign outside, they were also vendors of goods produced locally, particularly vegetables and fruits. (Courtesy Charles E. Petty.)

The Hulse-Walden home was built in 1903 on the south corner of Forest and Carolina Avenues. It was razed in 1972. The site is occupied today by a childcare center. (Courtesy North Augusta Historical Society.)

The Cleckley home was on Georgia Avenue near the present-day chamber of commerce. The Cleckley's were an early North Augusta family. William Cleckley was a town official and instrumental in the establishment of a cemetery in North Augusta, which at the time had now such facility. Cleckley was the first to be buried in Sunset Hill Cemetery. (Courtesy Marion B. Jones.)

This is the L. F. Verdery home, which was on Carolina Avenue. Leonard F. Verdery operated a poultry farm here in 1903. Many homes, such as this house, have been replaced by more-modern brick structures in various places throughout the city. (Courtesy North Augusta Historical Society.)

The Jacksons were members of Grace United Methodist Church, which was built on land donated by James U. Jackson and the North Augusta Land Company. (Courtesy North Augusta Historical Society.)

The Grace United Methodist Church parsonage, today a private residence, is located at the southeast corner of Forest and Georgia Avenues. (Courtesy Heritage Council of North Augusta.)

This photograph, probably taken around 1910–1914, shows a trolley headed up the hill on West Avenue toward the Hampton Terrace Hotel, whose smokestack can be seen in the distance. (Courtesy Charles E. Petty.)

An avid hunter James U. Jackson, pictured third from the left, and the party shown here may have been hunting locally or could have returned from Jackson's hunting preserve in Yemassee. The individual at the extreme left is wearing a uniform of a railroad employee suggesting a recent arrival by train. Many guests at the Hampton Terrace Hotel and local friends hunted with Jackson. It was a popular sport and one of his favorites. (Courtesy George Jackson Alexander.)

James U. Jackson's mother, Catherine Wyman Mixer Jackson, is buried in Augusta's Magnolia Cemetery. She was 17 years old when she and George Twiggs Jackson married in 1846; he was 24 years old. They had been married more than 50 years at his death in 1899. (Courtesy Heritage Council of North Augusta.)

Hampton Terrace from The Hill Augusta Ga. 1913

This photograph gives an idea of the impressive size of the Hampton Terrace Hotel—it is seen here from about a mile away. The rural scene in the foreground is in sharp contrast to the impressive structure on the hill in the background. (Courtesy Augusta Museum of History.)

Palmetto Lodge was originally built as a lodge for the Hampton Terrace Hotel. It became a private residence when purchased by New York residents the John Herberts. They were winter visitors, and Palmetto Lodge became the scene of much entertaining in the early 20th century. (Courtesy Heritage Council of North Augusta.)

This private residence on the southeast corner of Arlington Heights and Carolina Avenue was a tearoom operated by Mrs. Emery Platt Ruland. There was a paved walk from the hotel to the tearoom. (Courtesy Stan Byrdy.)

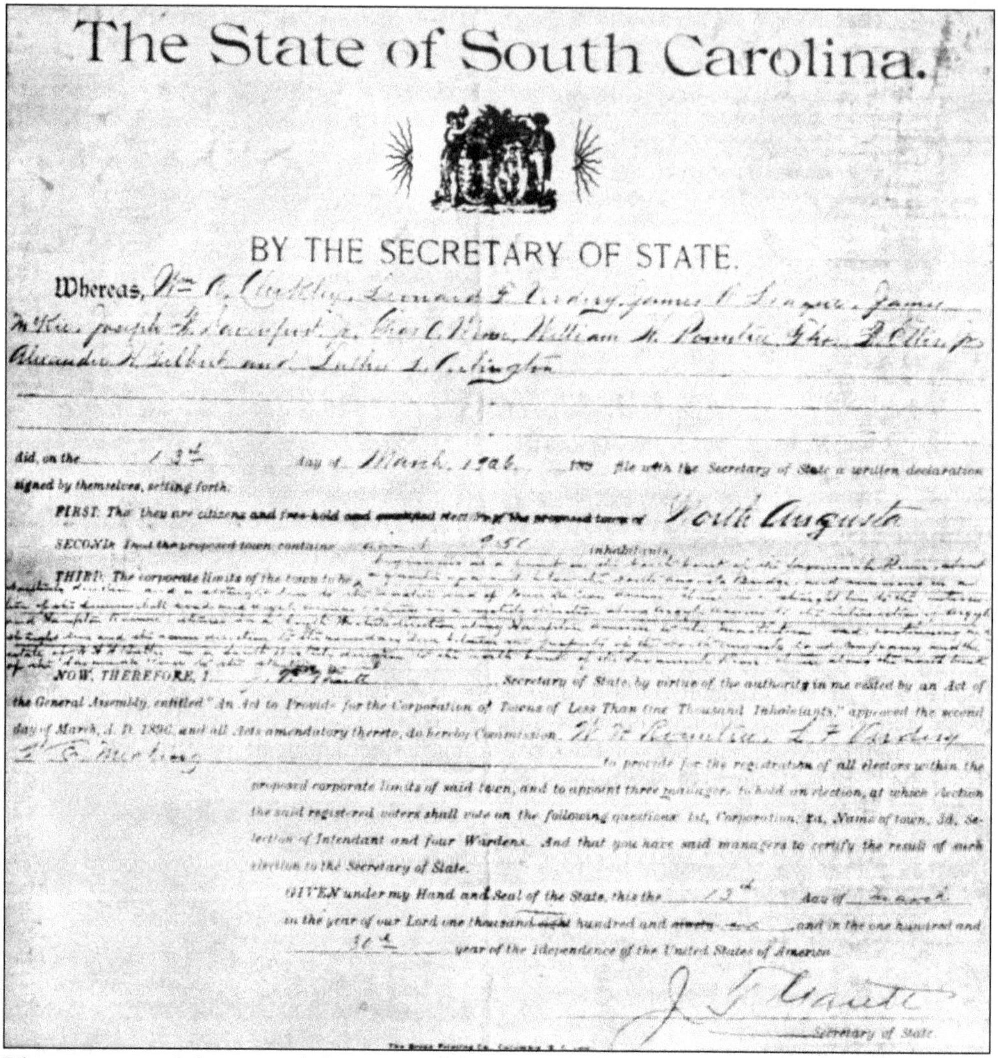
The State of South Carolina.

BY THE SECRETARY OF STATE.

Whereas,

did, on the 13th day of March, 1906, file with the Secretary of State a written declaration signed by themselves, setting forth:

FIRST: That they are citizens and free-hold and qualified electors of the proposed town of North Augusta

SECOND: That the proposed town contains about 250 inhabitants.

THIRD: The corporate limits of the town to be

NOW, THEREFORE, I, J. T. Gantt, Secretary of State, by virtue of the authority in me vested by an Act of the General Assembly, entitled "An Act to Provide for the Corporation of Towns of Less Than One Thousand Inhabitants," approved the second day of March, A. D. 1896, and all Acts amendatory thereto, do hereby Commission

to provide for the registration of all electors within the proposed corporate limits of said town, and to appoint three managers to hold an election, at which election the said registered voters shall vote on the following questions: 1st, Corporation; 2d, Name of town; 3d, Selection of Intendant and four Wardens. And that you have said managers to certify the result of such election to the Secretary of State.

GIVEN under my Hand and Seal of the State, this the 13th day of March in the year of our Lord one thousand nine hundred and six, and in the one hundred and 30th year of the Independence of the United States of America.

J. T. Gantt
Secretary of State.

This is a copy of the original document authorizing an election to be held for North Augusta to become a municipality. The city was granted a charter on April 11, 1906. (Courtesy City of North Augusta.)

Four

LIVING THE DREAM, SURVIVING THE NIGHTMARE 1907–1925

By the middle of 1907, all Augustans and North Augustans fully realized the value of the Augusta-Aiken Railway. However, it was not generally known that the line was a pioneer as an interurban electric railway in the South. Once more, James U. Jackson was praised for his ability, energy, and farsightedness, as the press and his contemporaries lauded him for his accomplishments and vision. The electric road made all the local markets more accessible. The growth was illustrated by the fact that a parcel express car did not earn enough in the first three months to cover the wages of the motorman and conductor; however, business grew so rapidly that in a few months a second express car, twice the size, was purchased. The two cars represented one third of the total revenue of the road. Farmers could get their produce to market with comparative ease. What once took a team and a driver a day with a wagon, the express car could deliver to market daily. Goods could be picked up at multiple locations along the line and delivered to market. Thus, individual did not loose a day's work in traveling to and from the market with their goods.

It had been proposed to extend the line to Columbia. The company bought a bridge over the Congaree River and surveyors were busy. Waterpower on the Saluda River had been purchased. By June 1907, the Augusta-Columbia Railway Company was ready to commence operations. Augusta and Columbia would be the terminal points of the new line. James U. Jackson was elected vice president of the new company. He was one of the youngest railroad officials in the country. Mr. W. T. Van Brunt was president of the conglomerate of the Augusta-Columbia Railway Company, Augusta Railway and Electric Company, Augusta-Aiken Railway Company, North Augusta Electric and Improvement Company, North Augusta Hotel Company, and the North Augusta Land Company. Mr. C. C. Tegethoff of New York was secretary and treasurer.

Town official William A. Cleckley had expressed a desire to be buried in North Augusta. Land was set aside for a city cemetery west of the city, off Buena Vista Avenue. Cleckley was the first to be buried there. Sunset Hill is where James U. Jackson and his wife, Edith, are buried. Expansion continued in the city. The Lamar home, built in 1907, stood on Georgia Avenue in what is today the Butler Avenue/Georgia Avenue Historic District. The home was destroyed by fire in the early 1930s. Two small brick houses occupy the site today. The home had been featured in an early movie, *The First Governor*, about an escaped Confederate prisoner of war.

A little farther down the hill on Georgia Avenue in the historic district is Pine Heights. It was built as a sanatorium for guests of the Hampton Terrace Hotel. In 1922, the Detroit Tigers used it while in Augusta for spring training. One of the two buildings of the complex was destroyed by fire in 1983. A Hampton Terrace Hotel register for 1907 found at Pine Heights lists Dr. R. E. Lee of Washington, son of Confederate general Robert E. Lee, as a guest.

In May 1907, James U. Jackson entertained his cousin, Marion Jackson Verdery, at an enjoyable stag supper. Guests included members of the Jackson and Verdery families and friend Jack Cranston. This was probably held at the Jackson home, but it might well have been at the Hampton Terrace Hotel. Edith and James were reported to have entertained at a bridge party, where at the conclusion of play, the eight tables of players were served a delicious supper.

During May 1907, a petition was filed in Columbia for the new county of Edisto. Jackson stated positively that this would not adversely affect the continued move for a new county with North Augusta as its county seat. Duncan Clinch Heyward was no longer governor of the state of South Carolina, but both he and Gov. Martin Frederick Ansel had appointed a commission for a new county with North Augusta as its county seat. At the end of June that year, South Carolina governor Ansel determined that the proposed new county was "the same" as the county of Heyward, which an election had rejected in December 1906. A meeting was called on June 29, 1907, at Jackson's office to discuss a response.

According to the *Augusta Chronicle,* in mid-July 1907, "a beautiful baby show" was held at the Jackson home on Carolina Avenue. The event, to benefit Grace United Methodist Church, was marked by "great beauty and social enjoyment." At the end of the month, the Jacksons entertained with a "typical country dance" in honor of their niece, Belle Vernon King of Rome, Georgia. The band played reels, and the ladies wore calico dresses. Ginger cake, lemonade, and striped candy were served to about 50 guests. It is difficult, at the beginning of the 21st century, to imagine the lifestyle of the Gilded Age.

The bridge across the Savannah River had been damaged as a result of a flood. In February 1908, there was a battle between the city (Augusta) and the Augusta-Aiken Railway Company in the matter of rebuilding the wrecked portion of the Thirteenth Street Bridge and the responsibility for such a repair. Augusta mayor William Dunbar held that the city was not, under the contract between the city and the railway, obligated to repair the bridge. James U. Jackson refused to listen; however, he was willing for a board of arbitrators to decide the matter. He indicated his company would donate a sum of not more than half the cost of repairs. The mayor vehemently opposed the idea. The North Augusta Land Company had conveyed the bridge to the city in June 1905. The city accepted the bridge and agreed to keep it open for travel; it had been agreed no toll would be charged, and if it ever were, the North Augusta Land Company would have free passage in perpetuity. Documents also stated the city would not be compelled to rebuild the bridge if freshets or high water destroyed it. Also in February 1908, meetings were held for the Augusta Railway and Electric Company and all the allied properties at the Hampton Terrace Hotel. Immediately following the meetings, a session of the board of directors was held. William Van Brunt would remain as president with Jackson as vice president and general manager. Boykin Wright would be general counsel and George T. Jackson associate counsel.

The following month, a Pullman train rolled into Union Station in Augusta with 175 members of the Cleveland Grays on board. The Cleveland Grays were formed in 1837 as a city guard and private militia. The group exists today. John D. Rockefeller, a former member of the group, was spending the winter in Augusta. He was on hand to meet them, as was James U. Jackson as president of the Augusta Railway and Electric Company. In Augusta, barbecue was served, and in the style of the period, the meal was eloquently described by the *Augusta Chronicle* as "succulent slices of crisp skinned pork, ravished by the seductive odor of steaming hash, the like of which had never been imagined in their most fanciful epicurean dreams." The party then went to the Hampton Terrace Hotel, where the ladies participated in an informal reception in the parlors, and the gentlemen were served refreshments in the café.

The matter of the new county continued. James Jackson offered to build a courthouse and jail for the new county at a cost of no less than $25,000. He continued to extol the merits of electric power by stating that 20 years or so earlier, the first attempt to run a streetcar by electricity was made. By 1890, the entire street railway of Augusta was changed from hay burners to electric. When Jackson first explored the idea of a trolley line, it was considered impossible to transmit a current any great distance. For that reason, it had been felt a trolley could only succeed in a thickly settled city. Soon it was found that, with substations, the current could be carried a considerable distance. When he decided to build an interurban road, many laughed at the proposal. Jackson was quick to point out that interurban roads were being constructed all over the world. He praised the fact that the Augusta Canal Company was able to furnish 12,000 horsepower to provide electricity after citizens in 1873 had authorized a bond issue. The revenues from those bonds had been more than sufficient to pay the interest, not just on those bonds but also on bonds issued for other purposes. James U. Jackson was truly a visionary; he dared to go where so many others would not. He felt the state of South Carolina should issue bonds to continue to progress. With the amount of waterpower available in the state and the ability to transfer current over great distances, he believed machinery could be used in rice fields. At the time, there were advocates of government ownership of railroads and utilities. Jackson did not approve of government ownership. It was reported in the *Augusta Chronicle* at the time of his plea to develop electric power "with Jim Jackson one success is only the stepping stone to another."

The matter of the bridge damaged by the flood of 1908 was resolved when Jackson signed and the city of Augusta approved an agreement to repair the bridge at once. A toll would be charged until the cost of repairs had been recovered. Jackson took exception to an article suggesting the financial status of the street railway was not good. He pointed out that the North Augusta Land Company, one of Jackson's companies, was a partner with the city of Augusta in matters concerning the bridge (having conveyed the bridge to Augusta in June 1905). The street railway had suffered, as had may tax payers, due to the flood. He asserted that the company's financial condition was not crippled. Later that month, Mayor Dunbar and Jackson were at odds again, this time over Augusta's lack of streetlights. Jackson explained the lack of water facilities was impacting the operation of the power plants. Not enough water was available to open the boilers now that the city was being furnished with steam-powered electric generators. He explained that while the plant was installing new machinery, the high water had caused breaks in the canal banks; the result was insufficient water to supply the boilers. In October, he went to New York to make arrangements to enlarge the power plant of the Augusta Railway and Electric Company. Jackson announced the closing of a deal between the North Augusta Investment Company and Twin City Power Company for two acres in North Augusta which the power company would use as a distribution point for the electricity they generated 30 miles up the Savannah River.

At a meeting of the chamber of commerce, a resolution was passed to invite president-elect William Howard Taft to visit Augusta during the winter. Jackson offered his home to the president-elect. Several telegrams were exchanged; it was decided the Hampton Terrace Hotel would open on December 15, beginning its winter season earlier than the usual date of January 5. The Bon Air Hotel would begin its season on December 17. On December 26, 1908, it was reported that president-elect William Howard Taft had spent a quiet Christmas day. During the afternoon, he had enjoyed a horseback ride. The party went out Washington Road and returned via Wrightsboro Road. His magnificent mount was from the Bon Air Hotel stables. Taft participated in the annual handicap golf tournament, which he won from Major Joseph B. Cumming of Augusta. On December 26, Taft and his family went with James U. Jackson and others on a trolley ride to Aiken. In early 1909, the president-elect was the guest of honor in Augusta. Although he had been a resident of the area for more than a month when Taft spoke at a speaker's stand at Broad Street and Jackson Street (today's Eighth Street), it was his first public address. The president-elect spoke at 4 p.m. James U. Jackson was one of those on the speaker's stand. After the address, special cars carried guests from Augusta to the Hampton Terrace Hotel for a banquet, after which the guests were taken, again in special cars, to Augusta, Summerville, and Aiken. Surely this must have been an occasion for James U. Jackson's beaver-skin top hat. A few days later, an 18-hole handicap golf tournament was held at the Hampton Terrace Hotel. The prize offered by W. B. Perry was a silver cup. Mr. Perry had the best score; the cup was presented to Jackson, who had the next best score. During this visit, president-elect William Howard Taft and his escorts traveled by automobile to the Beech Island Agricultural Club, crossing the Savannah River on the Sand Bar Ferry.

James U. Jackson, always seeking to improve or establish new businesses, went to New York to seek financing and returned in March indicating the Augusta-Aiken Railway would make improvements to the road and also purchase six new cars and straighten some sections of the line.

In August 1909, the chamber of commerce committee, including Jackson, went to Beverly, Massachusetts, to persuade President Taft to visit Augusta in November and open the fair. Augusta native Capt. Archibald Butt, military aide to President Taft, was a distant cousin of Thomas Loyless, editor of the *Augusta Chronicle*. Both he and the president's private secretary, Fred W. Carpenter, were very helpful in arranging an audience with Taft for the Augusta delegation. It was announced President Taft would open the Georgia-Carolina Fair on November 8. James U. Jackson, as president of the Georgia-Carolina Fair Association, joined the delegation, along with Thomas Loyless, Roy Goodwin, and T. J. Sheron. The president's schedule was arranged to enable him to go to Columbia on Saturday, visit Augusta on Sunday, stay until Monday, and go on to Wilmington by train.

In mid-August 1909, a committee of the Business Men's Club became incorporated as a stock company rather than asking businesses to donate money. The organization, it was felt, could be established simply by subscribing in stock. It was hoped Jackson would accept the position of secretary, which he did.

The Gilded Age was a time of social etiquette unfamiliar today. At Augusta's Academy of Richmond County in 1909, James and Edith's daughter, Edith, made use of dance cards, as was the custom of the time.

In December 1909, James U. Jackson retired as head of the Georgia-Carolina Fair Association, having served three terms. At the annual general meeting to elect a new board and other officers, the members were not able to persuade him to continue. M. E. Hennessy of the *Boston Globe*, who had been helpful to the chamber delegation the previous summer, visited Augusta in January 1910 and stayed at the Hampton Terrace Hotel.

On July 10, 1910, Governor Ansel of South Carolina appointed commissioners to again address the matter of a new county. The commission would then select surveyors and begin the process to submit an application to the governor to hold an election to approve a new county with North Augusta as the county seat, and as long as constitutional requirements were met, an election could be ordered. At this time, no name for the proposed new county had been selected.

At the end of 1910, with the street railway in new strong financial hands, Jackson announced improvements in power and additional lines. An extension to the city wharf to aid in the transfer of goods was planned. Electric lights and feeder lines on Broad Street would be put underground to enhance the streetscape. Machinery to add 3,000 horsepower to the capacity of the power plant would be installed.

On January 11, 1911, it was announced an election would be held on February 7 to vote on the matter of a new county. Again the proposal was defeated, primarily because the boundary lines drawn had a profound effect on Ellenton. In October, a new petition was presented to the new South Carolina governor Cole Blease. James U. Jackson met with Governor Blease on November 11, and a week later it was announced that the governor refused to entertain the petition and the entire matter would have to wait until after the session of the general assembly. During the previous session of the general assembly, a measure had been introduced aimed at "ill-formed" counties. It was generally felt that the proposed new county would come under that act. Jackson declared a new survey would be conducted to meet the criteria of the constitution, and the petition would be presented in 1912. If the general assembly passed the "ill-formed" county act, the matter of a new county would be lost.

Daniel Burns Dyer, pioneer of electric power in Augusta from whom Jackson had purchased the Augusta Railway and Electric Company in 1902, died in 1912, one year after returning to the plains of the West in a business partnership with old friend William F. "Buffalo Bill" Cody. Jackson had subsequently sold the trolley system to Edward Harriman, who in turn sold it to a group of northern investors. With the Augusta-Aiken Street Railway in Northern hands, the employees were not satisfied. A strike, prompted by the issue of low wages, occurred. After a great deal of controversy, during which time strikers tore up tracks and the National Guard was called to protect the power plant, the two sides reconciled.

In early 1912, James U. Jackson was accidentally shot while hunting on his game preserve near Yemassee. He was apparently shot in the face with birdshot from some distance. Several pieces of shot were lodged in the side of his face. He came back to North Augusta to have them removed and recuperate at home. The annual meeting of the allied street railway interests was held in April, and Vice President James U. Jackson presided. At the annual meetings of the other companies, the old boards were re-elected. Jackson was a representative on each.

Following another flood in 1912, the levee was extended. A further watery event in April of that year was the sinking of the ocean liner *Titanic*. Archie Butt, the military aide to President Taft, who had been so helpful to Jackson and the Augusta delegation when they went to Beverly, Massachusetts, in 1909, was lost when the liner sank. A memorial bridge over the Augusta canal would be dedicated to him by former president Taft in 1914.

In 1912, the Hampton Terrace Country Club was organized. James U. Jackson was named president of the club. The golf course and the tennis amenities of the Hampton Terrace Hotel would be free to members. At a dinner at the hotel, Jackson announced that some 200 people had been elected for membership. A special meeting was called a few days later for ladies who were interested. A mass meeting was held in August 1912 to endorse the candidacy of Sen. Benjamin Ryan Tillman for governor of South Carolina, to help "redeem the state from Bleaseism."

In June 1913, James and Edith's daughter, Edith, was married to James Bishop Alexander at the family home. According to reports, the Jackson home "resembled a fairy palace" with its brilliant illuminations. The 9 p.m. wedding was the social event of the season; each room of the home was filled with flowers and candles. The former pastor of Grace United Methodist Church, Rev. J. Le Max Stokes, performed the ceremony. The bride wrote to her parents from the Toxaway Inn in Upstate South Carolina, where she and her husband spent their honeymoon.

In January 1914, Walter, James U. Jackson's son by his first wife, Minnie, was married at the Sacred Heart Church parsonage. It was a small wedding at which the groom was attended by his uncle, Walter M. Jackson. A bungalow was to be constructed for them on West Avenue in North Augusta; until then, the newlyweds would be living on Ellis Street in Augusta with Mrs. Michael Sheehan. The North Augusta City Directory for 1918 lists 408 West Avenue as the home of Walter and his wife.

The announcement of the engagement of James and Edith's oldest daughter, Daisy King, was made in October 1915. She was to marry A. Baudry Moore of Savannah, son of Judge A. B. Moore. A wedding followed in December. The Jackson home was again ablaze with lights and filled with flowers for the 6:30 p.m. ceremony. Garlands of vines with tiny electric lights were hung between the huge columns of Rosemary Hall. This is the first time the Jackson home was referred to by the name we know it as today. It was named not for the rosemary pine, but for the rosemary planted in the garden.

James U. Jackson and his wife, Edith, went to Rome, Georgia, in December 1917 for the wedding of their son James U. Jackson Jr. to Lilla Fickling. It was reported the newlyweds would be with the family at Rosemary Hall for the Christmas season.

In January 1915, the North Augusta Water and Gas Company was chartered with a capital of $50,000 and James U. Jackson as president. In February, he was appointed industrial agent of the Augusta-Aiken Railway and Electric Company. The president, F. Q. Brown, made the announcement. James U. Jackson was to secure new industries and further the properties along the lines.

Jackson's cousin and older brother to Marion Jackson Verdery, George Jackson Verdery, died in April 1915. He had been named for James U. Jackson's father. The funeral service was held at Grace United Methodist Church, of which both Verdery and Jackson were members. Verdery had fought for the Confederacy during the War Between the States and served with Stonewall Jackson. At Stonewall Jackson's death, he served with Gen. Joe Johnston until Johnston surrendered in April 1865. Verdery had worked as custodian of the building and grounds of the Hampton Terrace Hotel from the time it was constructed. Among his children, four of the five girls married into well-known North Augusta families. Daughter Nina, North Augusta's first schoolteacher, was working in 1918 as a clerk at P. J. Berckman's nursery, which later became home to the Augusta National Golf Course and the annual Masters Golf Tournament. Members of the Verdery family continue to be a part of North Augusta and its history.

In the summer of 1916, it was announced that there was to be a local company to distribute "Motor-Vim," an energizing agent claimed to greatly increase mileage, give power to automotive engines, and remove carbon deposits from cylinders. The Augusta office would be the headquarters for 18 states. The company formed was Jackson and Cranston, founded by James U. Jackson and John M. Cranston. Jackson showed a number of testimonials from individuals, including Hollis Boardman. Hollis was a local entrepreneur who had worked for the Standard Oil Company, owned by John D. Rockefeller. He founded Peoples Oil Company in North Augusta in 1904.

In the fall of 1916, James U. Jackson returned from New York with several Augusta business associates. He had formed a syndicate to take over the Hampton Terrace Hotel and more than 5,000 acres of unimproved land in the area of Clearwater. Plans were to add a substantial number of new rooms to the resort hotel. Prominent in hotel circles, Mr. W. H. Barse, most recently at the Nassau in Long Beach, Long Island, would be the new lessee. Since its construction, the Hampton Terrace Hotel had several owners. John Skelton Williams and William Middendorf and Company took over the allied properties in 1903. Then came the Equitable Trust Company of Augusta; later Mr. Van Brunt, private secretary to E. H. Harriman and backed by Harriman, secured control. When Van Brunt and Harriman separated, Harriman took over, and the allied properties were part of his estate at the time of his death. Next the real estate was sold to White and Company, and it was from them James U. Jackson and his group purchased the property. After conceiving the idea of a resort hotel and bringing the project to a successful conclusion, James U. Jackson became an actual owner of the property. In a few months it would be reduced to underinsured ashes, but in the fall of 1916, James U. Jackson was congratulated on all sides for becoming the new owner of these most valuable properties.

On January 11, 1917, the annual convention of New York Life Insurance Company agents was to be held at the Hampton Terrace Hotel. Arrangements had been made for the opening of the famous hostelry on January 4. The new season was expected to be the biggest ever! Other conventions had been booked. The North Augusta Land Company had applied to the secretary of state of South Carolina for permission to increase its stock from $1 million to $1.5 million. Since the recent purchase, the North Augusta Land Company owned the hotel building, water works, and other property it had not previously owned.

The year of the Great Fire in Augusta was 1916. High winds destroyed some 526 homes and 138 businesses, including the Dyer Building, Augusta's first office building, where the fire started. SunTrust Bank is located on the site today. Other fires in later years claimed the Georgia Railroad offices and the Bon Air Hotel, but the fire on December 31, 1916, that destroyed the Hampton Terrace Hotel was a catastrophe. Purchased by James U. Jackson and associates only months before and totally renovated for another banner season, the Hampton Terrace Hotel was insured for $200,000. The property value was about $750,000. Previously coverage of $300,000 had been held on the property, but South Carolina law governing insurance had changed, and once enacted, it became difficult to maintain the insurance; as policies expired, companies declined to renew. The management had to seek coverage through New York brokers. General agents were Brown, Peck, Hughes, and Crosby in New York and Alex Goodwin Garrett in Augusta. The fire started in the west wing, smoldered, and then burst out, enveloping that entire section. To that point, it seemed the fire might be brought under control, but once it burst through the roof at about 3 a.m., it was unlikely the building could be saved. About 100 people were there at the time, various staff members working to ready the renovated hotel for the new season. Almost all the Augusta fire departments responded: Nos. 3, 4, 6, and 7 rushed to North Augusta; however, the location of the hotel high on the hill caused insufficient water pressure. Fireplugs at the location were without a standard fitting to couple to the hoses being used. It was reported those battling the blaze had insufficient water; they succeeded in getting three streams on, but the capacity of the equipment that responded was 10 streams—3,150 gallons a minute. Even with sufficient water, little could have been done. By 5 a.m., the fire moved through the main building toward the east wing. The fact that there was little or no wind saved North Augusta itself from destruction. Heat blistered nearby homes. Some furniture was saved, and today it can be found in the homes of James U. Jackson's grandchildren.

In January 1917, a week after the blaze, the citizens of North Augusta were ready to put up $50,000 for a new Hampton Terrace Hotel. James U. Jackson spoke to the mass meeting; his plan was that, with citizens' assistance, the municipality could vote $50,000 in bonds. After checking South Carolina law, he said the town could issue bonds amounting to eight percent of the town's taxable property. That taxable property being $880,000, eight percent would be $70,000. The lessee, W. H. Barse, spoke to the group. He indicated he and his wife had made all the arrangements necessary for their move to North Augusta, and he hoped that move would still be possible. Jackson set out the financial plan showing how the $50,000 bond issue would not have to be paid by North Augusta directly. It is not surprising that only one week after the tragedy he had a workable financial plan in place. At the beginning of February, detailed plans for rebuilding the Hampton Terrace Hotel were announced.

The South Carolina state insurance commissioner ordered his deputy insurance commissioner to make a full investigation. The cause for the fire was determined to be faulty wiring. The origin of the fire was in the area of Room 7 in the west wing, with the fire originating between the ceiling of the third floor and the floor of the fourth floor, or possibly between the inside walls and outside weatherboarding. When the Hampton Terrace Hotel was built in 1902, it was of ordinary frame construction; the walls were built without fire stops. The original wiring was in conduit; however, it was impossible to determine if additional wiring or wiring repair had been done in the area of the origin of the fire. The fact that no blowtorches were used to remove old paint and servants were cleaning up behind workmen eliminated the possibility of spontaneous combustion from oily rags or waste. Two watchmen were employed, and the hotel was equipped with fire extinguishers. Each hall had two lines of hose attached to water pipes. The water for fire protection was pumped from ponds into a standpipe 100 yards from the hotel. There were hydrants around the hotel, but the steep embankment made them inaccessible to pumping apparatus, or they were cut off from the street by cement pavements with elevated sides. The hoses could not be connected to outside hydrants, because the threads on the couplings were incompatible with those on the hydrants. The final conclusion was that defective wiring most probably caused the fire. Other defective wiring had been discovered and corrected in other parts of the building, but the inspectors had not yet reached the west wing. As sometimes occurs, it was a series of unfortunate circumstances and events that came together and caused the catastrophe.

James U. Jackson received telegrams from Caldwell and Sons of Louisville, Kentucky, informing him that Charles Caldwell, superintendent of construction for the company, would be in Augusta to begin the work of rebuilding the Hampton Terrace Hotel. Jackson flung himself into the rebuilding; fate however, had other plans. The total destruction of the resort hotel only months after James U. Jackson and his associates became owners was a nearly mortal blow. Then while returning from a business trip regarding the new Hampton Terrace Hotel, Jackson was in a railroad accident in North Carolina. The sleeper coach in which he was riding overturned, and he sustained a broken rib. His physician did not think he could keep him "in for long." Jackson conducted directors' meetings in his bedroom at Rosemary Hall.

The hand of fate was still looming large. There were many factors that made the rebuilding plans difficult. The timing for the Hampton Terrace Hotel rebuilding project was not the best. German U-boats were wreaking havoc on shipping, cotton prices were in flux, wheat was low, and money was tight. Still nothing deterred Jackson from going from city to city with broken bones and working day and night. The Hampton Terrace Hotel lessee, himself a tireless worker, was backed by Jackson at every turn. It was stated the new Hampton Terrace Hotel would be ready by the next season. A admirer of Jackson's said he was "as the squirrel you can't keep on the ground." There had been a possibility of a manufacturing plant for "golf sticks" being located in the Augusta area. Manufacturer Seamore Dunn had stayed at the Hampton Terrace Hotel and had told Jackson he planned to select a site in the area. It was not known if the Seamore Dunn plan would be abandoned.

James U. Jackson, at the pinnacle of his personal and financial success, was left, after the tragedy of the Hampton Terrace Hotel fire, with very little. His indomitable spirit kept rebuilding plans alive, but the financial climate of the time was not favorable. A cluster of homes, the remains of the smokestack, some of the basement area, and a section of sidewalk are all that remain today.

A meeting of the North Augusta Commission of Public Works was held in the summer of 1918. Jackson, the receiver of the waterworks system, offered to sell; the three commissioners, however, felt the price was too high. They declared their plan to go ahead with a new system. North Augusta had unanimously voted $50,000 in bonds to secure an adequate water supply. The commission declined to give the figure at which the receiver had offered the system.

In May 1920, James Jackson was named industrial agent of the Georgia Railroad, with offices in Augusta. One of his projects, in addition to securing industry, was to promote the development of navigation on the Savannah River.

In February 1922, the *Detroit Free Press* announced there was to be style and comfort for Ty Cobb and the Detroit Tigers during spring training in Augusta. They would be staying at Rosemary and Lookaway Halls, and Pine Heights was also to be used. Mr. and Mrs. James U. Jackson and Mr. and Mrs. George T. Jackson would occupy the Munnerlyn home, which can be seen today across from Rosemary Hall, at 825 Carolina Avenue, while the Detroit Tigers used their homes. President Harding watched Ty Cobb and Detroit in 1923 while staying at the rebuilt Bon Air Hotel.

The infestation of the boll weevil in 1921 and 1922 culminated in the almost total ruin of the cotton crop in 1923. A group of bankers and railroad contractors were in Edgefield in 1924, inspecting the proposed route of an extension of the Georgia Florida Railroad from Augusta to Greenwood via Edgefield. James U. Jackson, as the special representative of the Georgia Florida, was among the group.

Early in 1925, James U. Jackson was in Chicago in talks with Benjamin Marshall. Jackson, as joint owner and promoter of the North Augusta Land Company, was expected to announce the construction of a $4-million hotel and tourist colony development to be built on a 4,000 tract formerly belonging to the North Augusta Land Company. The location was about three miles beyond the Hampton Terrace Hotel site. All bedrooms would be outside rooms, and each would have four windows and a bath. There was to be a combination tropical garden and dining room, a dance floor, and a swimming pool with palm trees. Plans included a roof and walls that could be opened or closed as the weather dictated. There would be a polo field, aviation landing field, golf course, tennis courts, and a bridle path. Scheduled to begin construction in 10 days, the new hotel site would include a boulevard through Clearwater to link with the new hard-surface road to Aiken.

In February, Jackson addressed a meeting of the Kiwanis Club in Aiken with regard to the future of the proposed new hotel. He had made a similar presentation to the Aiken Chamber of Commerce in January. Son-in-law J. Bishop Alexander and son John Williams Jackson went with him when he made the presentations. In May, James U. Jackson was responsible for the Georgia Florida Railroad Exhibit at the Southern Exposition in New York. He was highly praised by the editor of the *Manufacturing Record* of Baltimore. He had worked eight years on a plan to rebuild the Hampton Terrace Hotel, and finally, a little more than six months before his death, a deal was made. Work was to begin the next week—what happened? Benjamin Marshall's plan never materialized, and nothing more was heard about the project. Sketches of the proposed hotel were featured in the *Augusta Chronicle*.

After a relatively short illness, James U. Jackson died on October 15, 1925. Described in the *Augusta Chronicle* "as a dreamer and master builder," he was both, and he made his dreams come true. Marion Jackson Verdery was among the pallbearers. The funeral was at the Jackson home, Rosemary Hall, with the service conducted by the Reverend T. C. O'Dell of Grace United Methodist Church. Although he had been quite ill and was not expected to recover, his death nevertheless came as a great shock. Anyone who ever knew him hoped his indomitable spirit would prevail.

Although he had been involved in a number of projects after the loss of the Hampton Terrace Hotel, James U. Jackson never regained the momentum he had prior to that event. He was buried in the family lot in Sunset Hill Cemetery. It would be 30 years before Edith took her place there beside him. Floods again in 1925 wreaked havoc along the river.

There was extensive damage to the North Augusta Bridge after the flood of 1908. There was a great deal of discussion between Augusta and James U. Jackson representing the North Augusta Land Company as to who held responsibility for repairs and the financial cost of those repairs. An agreement was reached by which a toll would be charged to cover repairs. (Above courtesy Augusta Richmond County Historical Society, Reese Library, Augusta State University. Below courtesy North Augusta Historical Society.)

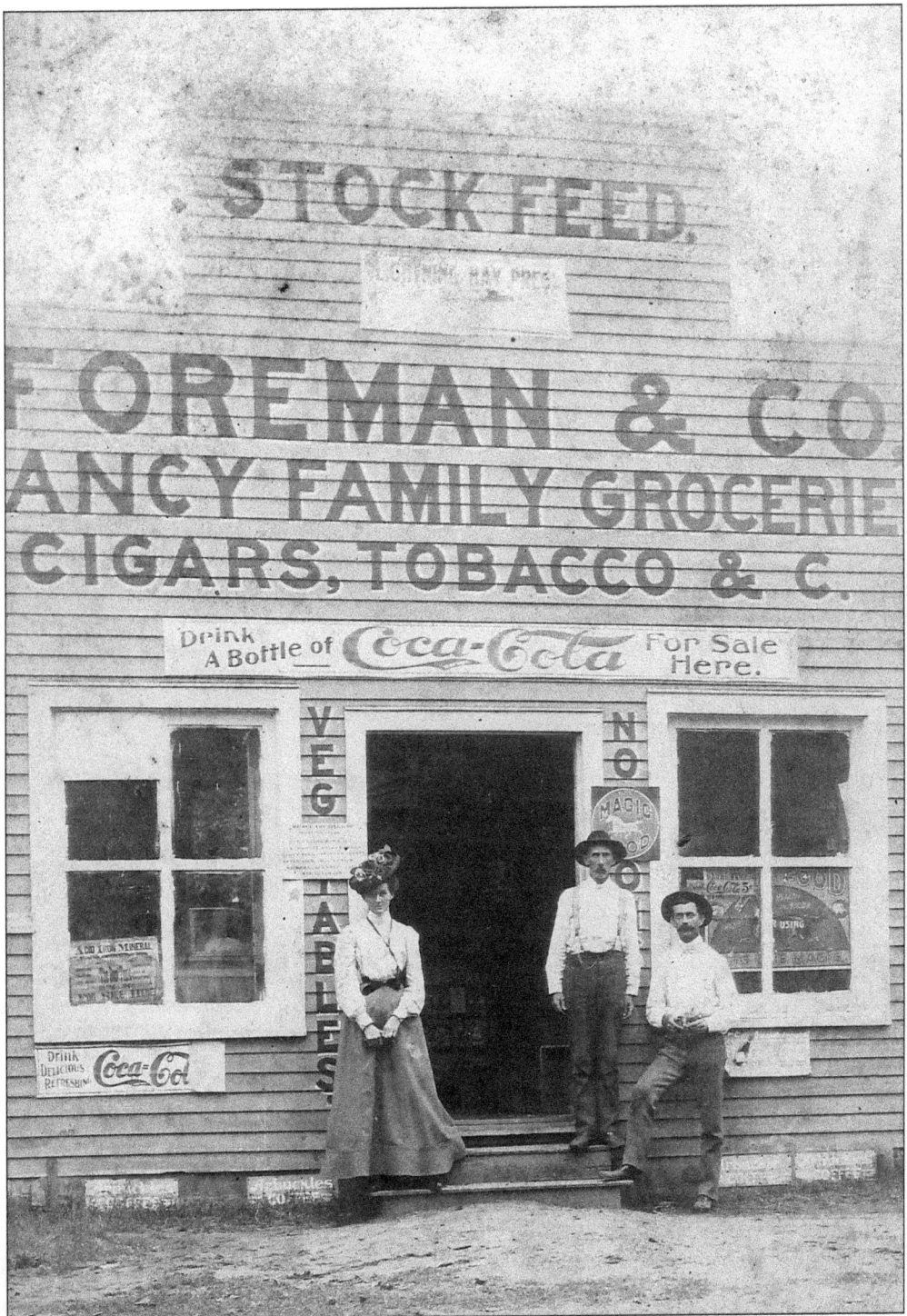

Foreman's store was an early North Augusta business. They established other businesses in the city, including a Ford dealership on Georgia Avenue. (Courtesy Charles E. Petty.)

The interurban road revolutionized the movement of goods to market. One of the freight cars of the Augusta-Aiken Railway is pictured here. (Courtesy North Augusta Historical Society.)

PINE HEIGHTS SANATORIUM, NORTH AUGUSTA, S C.

Pine Heights was built about the same time as the Hampton Terrace Hotel. It was designed to serve as a sanatorium for hotel guests. (Courtesy Dr. Joe Holt.)

Today Pine Heights is home to the Family Center. When the buildings were divided into apartments in 1983, a fire in the lower building caused it to be destroyed. (Photograph Heritage Council of North Augusta. Courtesy Dr. Joe Holt.)

The Lamar home was on the hill on Georgia Avenue in what today is the Georgia Avenue/Butler Avenue Historic District. It was damaged by fire in 1931 and was demolished. (Courtesy North Augusta Historical Society.)

This is a photograph of the approach to the Thirteenth Street Bridge on Georgia Avenue, taken around 1914. The bridge had been repaved after the 1908 flood and was rebuilt in 1939 and again in 1972. (Courtesy Charles E. Petty.)

During his stay in Augusta in the winter of 1908–1909 and prior to his inauguration, president-elect William Howard Taft spoke in Augusta. This is a stereoscope image of that occasion. (Courtesy Augusta Museum of History.)

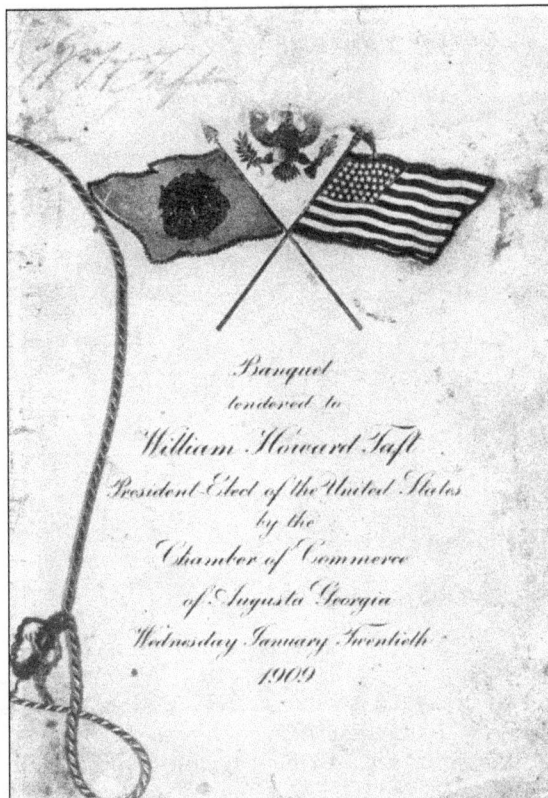

Renowned as a gourmet, Taft was honored at a banquet held at the Hampton Terrace Hotel. The menu was gastronomically suited to a man of William Howard Taft's tastes. This program was autographed by him on that occasion. (Courtesy North Augusta Historical Society.)

James U. Jackson most probably wore his beaver-skin top hat, usually stored in a leather hatbox, at various events during president-elect William Howard Taft's visit to Augusta. (Courtesy George Jackson Alexander.)

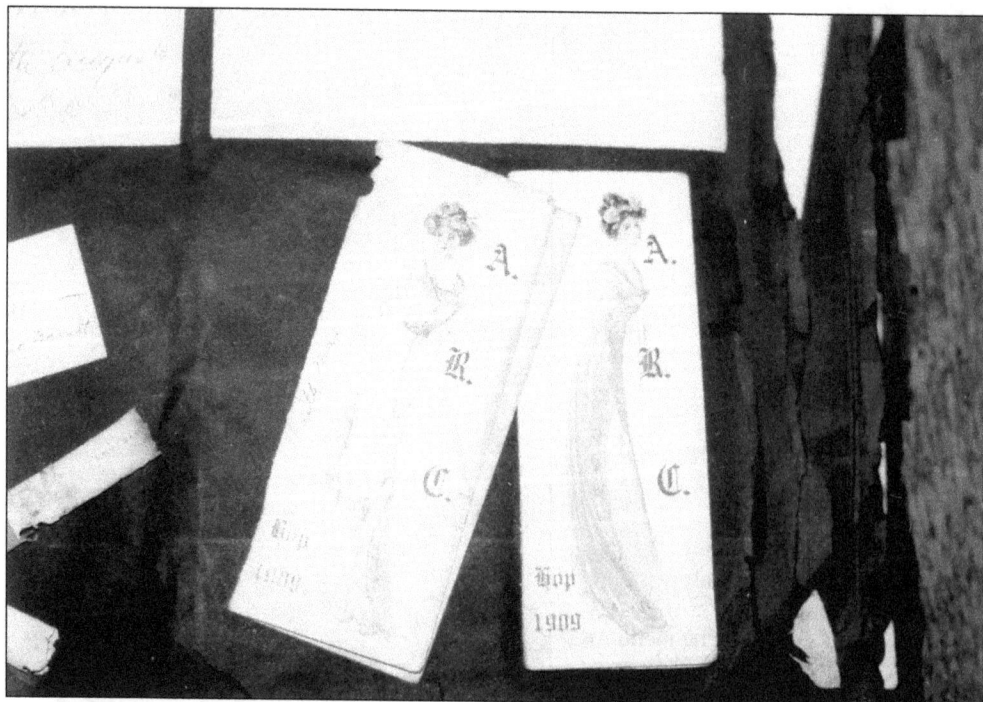

James U. Jackson's daughter, Edith, used these dance cards at the Academy of Richmond County in 1909 when she was about 16 years old. Dance cards were customary among the wealthier classes in the Gilded Age. (Courtesy George Jackson Alexander.)

President-elect William Howard Taft is seen leaving the Bon Air Hotel and crossing the Savannah River on the Sand Bar Ferry to visit the prestigious Beech Island Agricultural Club. Established in 1856 by South Carolina governor James H. Hammond, members of the Beech Island Agricultural Club still meet on the first Saturday of each month. (Courtesy Beech Island Agricultural Club.)

Pictured here is the Southern Railway Depot. Southern Railway serviced trains in the repair shops at Hamburg. It later became the location for Hamburg Industries. Today TTX Company–SRD–Hamburg Division operates a major contract railroad car repair shop at the site. (Courtesy Charles E. Petty.)

Hampton Terrace,
Augusta, Ga.

In this view, a man can be seen walking up the hill to the Hampton Terrace Hotel. In the distance are two figures to the right of a group of pine trees. The caption at the bottom of the postcard is Hampton Terrace, Augusta, Georgia. (Courtesy Milledge G. Murray Collection)

An unidentified lady waits at the foyer entrance to the Hampton Terrace Hotel in 1910. The glass-enclosed area was sometimes used for parties. (Courtesy Augusta Museum of History.)

Part of the Hampton Terrace golf course is pictured here in 1910. Its open vista is very different to the courses of today in this country. The par 5 second hole had three bunkers and was 593 yards long. (Courtesy Joseph M. Lee III.)

An aide to both Presidents Teddy Roosevelt and Taft, Archibald Butt was honored in 1914 when President Taft dedicated the Butt Memorial Bridge to him. Butt was lost when the ocean liner *Titanic* sank in 1912. (Courtesy Augusta Canal Authority.)

The Butt Memorial Bridge can be seen today as it spans the Augusta Canal at Fifteenth Street. Archibald Butt was a distant cousin to Thomas Loyless, editor of the *Augusta Chronicle*. (Photograph Heritage Council of North Augusta. Courtesy Augusta Canal Authority.)

The flood of 1914 caused significant damage. Businesses along the river were flooded. Continual flooding problems eventually caused the demise of the riverfront area. Today, due to the dam on Lake Thurmond, water levels are regulated. (Courtesy North Augusta Historical Society. Courtesy Charles E. Petty.)

Harvey, Ida May, b 52 Main

Harvey, Dorothy, b 52 Main

Hayden, Ernest A (Virginia), treas J B White & Co, h 163 Jackson W.

Haynes, Stanley R (Martha), tel opr Postal, h 562 Georgia

Haynes, Stanley R, Jr, b 562 Georgia

Henderson, Lydia, farmer, h 11 Clifton

Henderson, Rosa, student, b 11 Clifton

Hill, Paul (Sarah), slsmn Smith Bros, h 454 West, ph 3335-J

Hill, Estelle, b 454 West

Hill, Annie Wright, student, b 454 West

Hill, Geo W, wks Ex Cooperage Co, b P Dill

Hitt, Pierce Y (Mae), car bldg Ga R R, h 315 West

Hildebrand, Samuel F (Claudia), naturalist, h 604 West

Hill, James L (Annie), rec tel Merchants Bk, b 573 Carolina

Hill, Carolyn, student, b 651 Lake

Hill, Martha, student, b 651 Lake

Hill, Wilber D (Daisy), tel opr Postal, h 651 Lake

Hiller, Eugene, carpenter, h 306 West

Hobbs, Hattie, Mrs, steno, b 605 West

Holley, Norton (Hattie), financial clk U S Arsenal, h 461 West

Holley, Julia May, student, b 461 West

Holley, Bessie Louise, student, b 461 West

Holley, Harry Norton, student, b 46, West

Holley, Russell Tillman, student, b 461 West

Holley, Julian Heyward, student, b 461 West

*Holmes, Press, caretaker Palmetto Lodge, h rear same

*Holmes, Lula, domestic Palmetto Lodge, h rear same

*Holmes, Emma, b Lula Holmes

*Holsty, Augustus (Carrie), laborer, h Whatley's Alley

Howard, Geo J (Annie May), trv slsmn, h 619 West, Tel 1750-J

Howard, Geo J, Jr, student, b 619 West

Howard, Sue, student, b 619 West

Hudson, Lula, laundress, h 6 Main

Hummel, Mrs Margaret, h 257 West

Humphreys, Alfred W (Emma), photogr, soft drinks, 4 Georgia

Hunter, Wm N, mgr Woolworth's, h 654 West

Hunter, Mrs Laura F, b 654 West

J

Jackson, Jas U (Edith B), Pres N A Land Co, h 550 Carolina, Tel. 371

Jackson, Jas U, Jr, student, b 550 Carolina

Jackson, Geo T (Willie Belle), atty, h 3 Forest, Tel. 1623-J

Jackson, Walter M, real estate, b 3 Forest

Jackson, Walter M, Jr (Cecilia), N A Ld Co, h 408 W, ph 1843-W

Jackson, Dewry C (Mary Frances), optician, h 858 Summerhill rd

On this page of the North Augusta City Directory for 1918, the Jackson family is listed, including James U. Jackson, wife Edith, and son James U. Jr. (Courtesy North Augusta Historical Society.)

CENTRAL FISH MARKET

Wholesale and Retail
FISH AND OYSTERS

217 Campbell Street   Phone 1246

*Turner, Mamie, domestic, h near Company's Barn
*Twiggs, Sallie, domestic, h 1 Knitting Mill
*Twiggs, Hattie, domestic, h 1 Knitting Mill
*Twiggs, Gussie, student, h 1 Knitting Mill
*Twiggs, Chris (Georgia), farmer, h Jackson W
*Twiggs, Sam, laborer, b Jackson W
*Twiggs, John, laborer, b Jackson W
*Twiggs, Hez (Pinkey), farmer, 103 Jackson W
Tyler, Mrs Jane E, b 350 West
Tyler, Milton L (Ruth), mgr Bk of Western Carolina, h 604
    Georgia, phone 1760-W
Tyler, Ruth, student, b 604 Georgia
Tyler, Mildred, student, b 604 Georgia
Tyler, Ida, student, b 604 Georgia
Tyler, Milton L Jr, student, b 604 Georgia
Tyler, Mrs Kate E (widow), h 551 Georgia
Tyler, Fred, student, b 551 Georgia
Tyler, Lavinia, student, b 551 Georgia

V

Veneer Co, The Augusta; C P Mulherin, mgr, 2 R R Ave, ph 809
Verdery, Mrs Georgia (widow), h 13 Woodlawn
Verdery, Mandose, shipg clk J B White, b 13 Woodlawn
Verdery, Harry, Pressing Club, h 606 Georgia
Vedrery, Eleanor, student, b 606 Georgia
Verdery, Horace H (Minnie), clk Willet Seed Co, h 504 Carolina
Verdery, Mrs Henrietta, phone 1843-J, h 400 West
Verdery, Leila, b 610 Georgia
Verdery, Nina, steno bkpr P J Berckmans Co, b 400 West
Vincent, Wm H (Amy D), audit Ga R R (ph 3378), h 564 Carolina
Vincent, Amy, student, b 564 Carolina
Vincent, Helen G, student, b 564 Carolina
Vincent, Katherine, student, b 564 Carolina

W

Wages, Chas C (Mabel), repr Manning Co, h 501 West
Wages, Chas Jr, student, b 501 West
Wages, Jack, student, b 501 West
Wages, Nellie, student, b 501 West
Walden, Andrew A (Ella), physn, ph 1835-J, h 508 Carolina
*Walker, Preston (Fannie), farmer, h West Jackson Ave
Walker, Henry P (Emeva), transfer agt C & W C, ph 1643-J,
    h 564 Georgia
Walker, Wm H (Fannie), bkpr J Willie Levy Co, ph 2149-J,
    h 855 Georgia
Walker, May, b 855 Georgia

Maxwell Brothers

PHONE 836

FURNITURE

973 BROAD STREET

Members of the Verdery family are listed here in the North Augusta City Directory for 1918, including Nina, was working as a bookkeeper at the time. (Courtesy North Augusta Historical Society.)

Mrs. George Jackson Verdery is shown here sitting on her porch at her home on West Avenue. Among the five daughters she and George had, Nina became North Augusta's first school teacher. (Courtesy North Augusta Historical Society.)

This is a photograph of the west wing of the Hampton Terrace Hotel in 1916 where the fire started. Apparently caused by faulty wiring, the blaze spread uncontrollably. (Courtesy Joseph M. Lee III.)

HAMPTON TERRACE

BURNED DEC 31 1916

Another view of the hotel's west wing shows its fire escapes, which were ironically never used during the blaze that started close by. Compounded by a series of unfortunate circumstances, the hotel burned to the ground. It had been recently renovated and insured for a fraction of its value, and the structure was a total loss. (Courtesy Augusta Museum of History.)

The Great Fire in Augusta took place on March 22, 1916. The conflagration caused hundreds of homes and businesses to be lost. Some of the devastation can be seen here. The fire started in the Dyer Building, Augusta's first office building, where at the turn of the century James U. Jackson and his nephew, George, had their offices. (Courtesy Charles E. Petty.)

Some furniture was saved from the fire at the Hampton Terrace Hotel in 1916. Two items are shown here: a library chair (one of a pair) and an iron stand proclaiming five o'clock tea. Both items shown here are in the homes of James U. Jackson's grandchildren. (Courtesy Hazel Jackson Boyles. Courtesy George Jackson Alexander.)

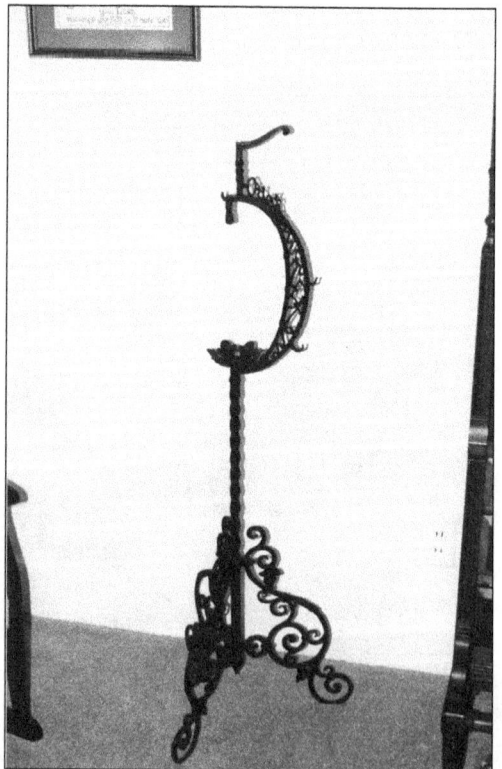

On the morning after the devastating fire, James U. Jackson walks among the ruins. The hotel, said to have been the largest wooden structure in the world at the time of its construction in 1903, was totally destroyed. (Courtesy North Augusta Historical Society.)

A pumper, similar to the one shown here, probably answered the call to the fire at the Hampton Terrace Hotel and was used to force water into a stream under pressure. (Courtesy North Augusta Historical Society.)

This photograph shows the ruins of the Hampton Terrace Hotel. There is nothing left of the once-magnificent building to identify which part is pictured. (Courtesy North Augusta Historical Society.)

These are the brick remains of the smokestack of the Hampton Terrace Hotel. They can be seen on Butler Avenue, across from Fairview Presbyterian Church. (Courtesy Stan Byrdy.)

The first page of the North Augusta City Directory for 1918 describes the city as a growing and progressive town on the high hills of South Carolina, connected by a steel bridge to Augusta, Georgia. It also describes the city's automobile turnpike, electric railway, waterworks, and electric lights. (Courtesy North Augusta Historical Society.)

NORTH AUGUSTA

CITY GUIDE

1918

MISCELLANEOUS INFORMATION

NORTH AUGUSTA, SOUTH CAROLINA

A growing and progressive town on the high hills of South Carolina, opposite Augusta, Ga. Noted for its healthful climate, and unsurpassed view for beauty. Connected with Augusta, Ga., by steel bridge, automobile turnpike, electric railway, telephone, etc. The town is well provided with waterworks, electric lights, sewerage, 15-minute car schedule to union station in Augusta, telephone, etc.

Two splendid school buildings and a public library. It is connected with Aiken, S. C. (the county seat), by electric railway. Cars run each way every hour.

Schultz High School and North Augusta Grammar School and two churches—Methodist and Baptist—furnish the intellectual and spiritual privileges of the town.

North Augusta is largely a residence and school town, yet it has a bank, cotton ginnery, cotton warehouse, lumber plant, box and crate works, veneer plant, cotton refining company, post-office, pottery, grist mill, automobile repair shops, blacksmith and wheelwright shops, several grocery and supply stores, hotel, floral gardens and bathing pond, the water of which is unequalled for its purity.

DETROIT
BASE BALL CLUB

SOUTHERN TRAINING
QUARTERS

AUGUSTA, GEORGIA.

The Detroit Tigers baseball team, with Ty Cobb, held their spring training in Augusta. In 1922 and 1923, they stayed at Lookaway and Rosemary Halls, homes of James U. and George T. Jackson. This is the stationery used by the Detroit Base Ball Club during summer training. Cobb owned a home in the Summerville area of Georgia. (Courtesy North Augusta Historical Society.)

It is not known when this photograph of James U. Jackson was taken. The trimmer moustache and studio photograph would suggest this was taken around the time North Augusta was granted its charter and became a municipality. James U. Jackson would be about 50 years old. (Courtesy George Jackson Alexander.)

This photograph of Mrs. James U. Jackson (Edith) was probably taken at her home, Rosemary Hall, where she lived until her death in 1955. Edith Jackson lived until the age of 90. This portrait would appear to have been taken when she was about 75, probably in 1940. (Courtesy North Augusta Historical Society.)

James Urquhart Jackson is pictured here. (Courtesy Hazel Jackson Boyles.)

James U. Jackson's grave in Sunset Hill Cemetery in North Augusta belies his importance in the history of the community. (Courtesy Heritage Council of North Augusta.)

This is the Jackson family plot in Sunset Hill Cemetery. Ornamentation on the column has been lost in recent years. James U. Jackson and his wife, Edith Barrington, are buried here, as is his son, John Williams; daughter Edith Barrington; her husband, J. Bishop Alexander; granddaughter Edith Barrington, wife of Dabney Harrison; grandson J. Bishop Alexander III; his wife, Elizabeth; and her sister, Jewell Huggins. James U. Jackson's nephew, George T. and his wife, Willie Belle, are adjacent to the plot. (Courtesy Heritage Council of North Augusta.)

This photograph shows the damage caused by the flood of 1925. The road is washed away, and the power poles knocked down. The flood of 1925 was significant in the amount of damage caused. Properties along the river never recovered. It was essentially the end of the riverfront business district. (Courtesy North Augusta Historical Society.)

Five

THE DREAM LIVES ON
1926

Immediately following James U. Jackson's death in 1925, meetings were held to determine a suitable permanent memorial. Naming the bridge across the Savannah River at Thirteenth Street in his honor was generally felt to be the most appropriate tribute; however, the floods of 1925 had caused significant damage to the bridge. The fact that the bridge itself was the property of the city of Augusta also presented problems. The Jackson Memorial Association was formed in March 1926. Discussion continued over the years. Again in 1929, the bridge was practically destroyed by yet another flood. The bridge was remodeled and rebuilt in 1939. It was officially named the James U. Jackson Memorial Bridge, and a bronze marker was placed there. The inscription read as follows:

> Jackson Memorial Bridge, built in 1890, to promote the founding and development of North Augusta by James U. Jackson, 1859–1925. A dreamer who made his dreams come true. In his honor and as a tribute to his unfaltering courage in the performance of many civic services this tablet is placed by the people of Augusta and North Augusta.

There appear to be differences in dates compared to other records; James U. Jackson's birth year is shown as 1859 rather than the correct date of 1856. Unfortunately the marker was stolen a few years later, during World War II. Finally in 1972, the bridge was rededicated and the present marker erected.

Marion Jackson Verdery died a year after James U. Jackson; James's brothers had all preceded him in death. Jackson's sister, Fanny, died in 1929, having lived all her life at the family home in Harrisonville. Sister Leila died in 1937.

In February 1926, at a meeting of the stockholders of the North Augusta Land Company, Benjamin Marshall of Chicago was elected president to succeed James U. Jackson, and Jackson's son, John, was elected to the board. A meeting was held at Rosemary Hall, at which time the matter of titles to the property was handled. Marshall had toured the area of the proposed colonial hotel and bungalow resort and its first golf course site before leaving to return north. It appeared the project Jackson had talked so much about in the months before his death would finally take shape.

Jim Jackson's youngest son, John Williams Jackson, was married in 1928 to Caroline Best. James U. Jackson Jr. was his brother's best man, and the couple was to live with him at Forest Hills on their return from their "wedding journey." Both Jackson's widow and his daughter, Edith, were wearing black at the ceremony, as they were still in mourning for their husband and father. It was announced a couple of months later that James U. Jackson Jr. and his wife were moving into an apartment at Rosemary Hall. In the fall of 1928, James Jr. was among those honored at a banquet for salesmen with Augusta Chevrolet distributor Henry Darling Inc. In 1929, Georgia Railroad Bank and Trust Company added the trust service, just as James Jackson had hoped for a few years earlier when he had to go out of town to seek financing.

Georgia Power was formed from several regional companies in 1927. The Georgia and Alabama Power Company took over the Augusta-Aiken Railway and Electric Company and the old power plant at Fifteenth Street in 1928. The vision Jim Jackson had with regard to the importance of electric power when he had put together a purchasing syndicate in Baltimore and New York proved to be valid. The group that had bought the Augusta Railway and Electric Company from Daniel Burns Dyer in 1902—Williams, Middendorf, MacAfee, Elliott, and James U. Jackson—envisioned the future. Dyer himself, who had lived on the plains of the West, came to Augusta acting as principal for a group of Kansas City businessmen who sensed the future of electric power and were interested in investing in electric development. Georgia Power had no use for the trolley line, and it was closed. The final run of the interurban railway was in 1929. George T. Jackson, nephew of James U. Jackson, was one of the few that had participated in the first trip in 1902 to make the memorable last journey.

At that time, in 1902, most people had not even dreamed of paved highways and certainly not thousands of cars traveling those highways. There was to be a bus service between Augusta and Aiken. With long-distance buses and airplanes bridging hundreds and thousands of miles in a few hours, there had been many changes. Mass-produced automobiles whose cost put them within the reach of many families were another factor changing the face of travel. The Roaring Twenties ushered in a new era, and the Gilded Age was gone. As to what happened to the proposed resort; perhaps it fell victim to progress? This question has never been answered. A viable proposal for the resort with architectural images in the form of sketches were shown in the *Augusta Chronicle*. Contracts were reportedly exchanged that developer Benjamin Marshall was to return in 10 days. Then nothing.

Repeated floods damaged the Thirteenth Street Bridge many times. It was rebuilt and dedicated to James U. Jackson in 1939. The present marker was erected in 1972 at a rededication ceremony attended by Jackson's daughter Edith (pictured third from the left) and son John (fourth from the left). Seventy years earlier, John had turned the ceremonial shovel of dirt to begin construction of the great Hampton Terrace Hotel. (Courtesy North Augusta Historical Society.)

The power plant at the canal and Fifteenth Street became the property of the Georgia Power Company when they bought the Augusta-Aiken Railway and Electric Company in 1928. (Courtesy Augusta Museum of History.)

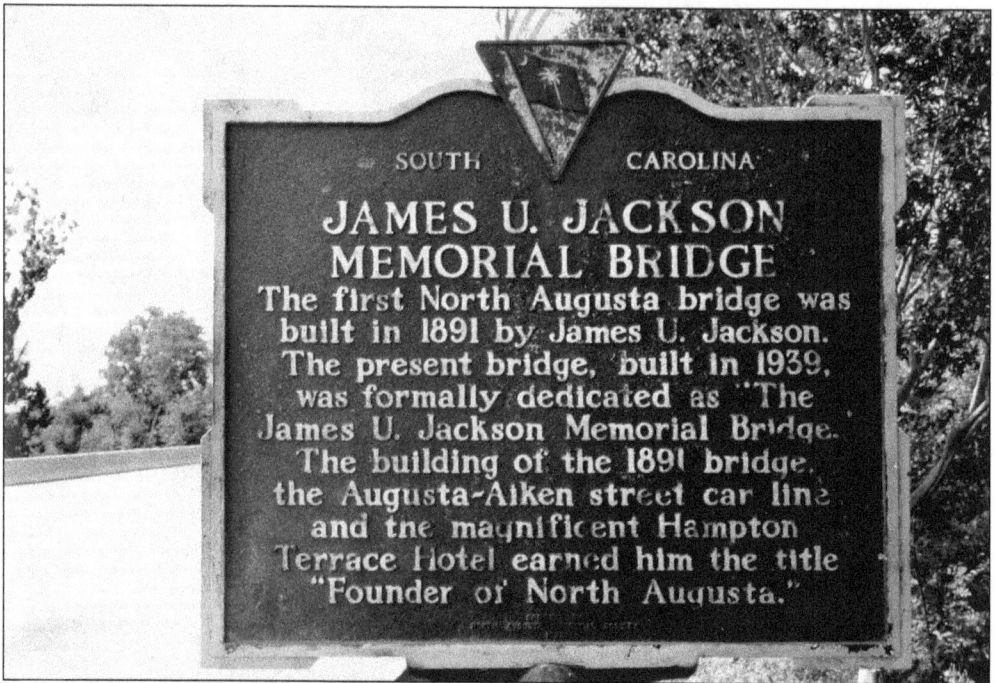

This historic marker can be seen on the James U. Jackson Memorial Bridge listing the accomplishments of James U. Jackson as the founder of North Augusta. First was the building of the bridge in 1891; the Augusta-Aiken Railway and the Hampton Terrace Hotel followed. As a prominent railroad executive, he secured Union Station in Augusta (Courtesy Heritage Council of North Augusta.)

The final run of the trolley was in 1929. Automobiles brought a major shift in transportation, and the glory days of the Augusta-Aiken Railway were over. (Courtesy North Augusta Historical Society.)

The Ladies Aid Society of Grace United Methodist Church is pictured here in 1929. Seated at left Mrs. James U. Jackson (Edith); fourth from right, in front of the mantel, is Mrs. George T. Jackson (Willie Belle). (Courtesy North Augusta Historical Society.)

James U. Jackson's grandson, George Jackson Alexander, was present at the dedication of the marker in 2000 honoring the Hampton Terrace Hotel's place in the history of North Augusta. (Courtesy Heritage Council of North Augusta.)

George Jackson "Jack" Alexander and his wife, Donna, are pictured on the porch of Lookaway Hall during the Hampton Terrace Days Festival of 2000. The festival was held for three years. (Courtesy George Jackson Alexander.)

EPILOGUE

A newspaper editorial at the time of the death of James U. Jackson stated in part: "James U. Jackson was a man with vision, a man who built great communities in his mind and whose dreams came true. He overcame obstacles that ofttimes seemed insuperable, a man of tireless energy and unfaltering faith such was James U. Jackson."

Eighty years have passed since North Augusta's founder left his legacy. He would be proud of his city and its progress. The city continues to pursue the vision, and the dream lives on. As part of the Hampton Terrace Days Festival in 2000, The Heritage Council of North Augusta dedicated a marker to the Hampton Terrace Hotel. The marker is located on Carolina Avenue at the foot of the hill where the imposing structure stood. A dam at Thurmond Lake controls the flow of water along the Savannah River. This beautiful city with its tree-lined streets and parks has new riverfront development. Today there is a different electric highway, but whatever the technology, the dream begins in the mind of the dreamer.

BIBLIOGRAPHY

1850 Richmond County, Georgia Census. Genealogical Enterprises, 1968.

Augusta, Georgia City Directory: Including Lakemont, Georgia and North Augusta, South Carolina. Richmond, VA: R. Polk Company, 1861.

Augusta, Georgia City Directory: Including Lakemont, Georgia and North Augusta, South Carolina. Richmond, VA: R. Polk Company, 1888–1889.

Augusta, Georgia City Directory: Including Lakemont, Georgia and North Augusta, South Carolina. Richmond, VA: R. Polk Company, 1891–1893.

Augusta Chronicle, Online Archives.

Callahan, Helen. *Augusta: A Pictorial History*. Virginia Beach: The Donning Company, 1980.

Cashin, Edward J. *The Story of Augusta*. Spartanburg, SC: The Reprint Company, 1996.

———. *The Brightest Arm of the Savannah: The Augusta Canal, 1845–2000*. Augusta, GA: Augusta Canal Authority, 2002.

Corley, Florence Fleming. *Confederate City*. Columbia, SC: USC Press, 1960.

Cumming, Mary G. Smith. *Two Centuries of Augusta*. Augusta, GA: Walton Printing Company, 1926.

Greene, Vicki H., Scott W. Loehr, and Erick D. Montgomery. *An Augusta Scrapbook: 20th Century Memories*. Charleston, SC: Arcadia Publishing, 2000.

History of North Augusta, South Carolina. Marceline, KS: Walsworth Publishing Company, 1980.

Jones, Chas. C. Jr., Salem Dutcher. *Memorial History of Augusta, Georgia*. Spartanburg, SC: Reprint Company, 1980.

McDowell, Dorothy Kelly. *An Aiken Scrapbook, Volume II*. Aiken, SC: Self-published, 1982.

North Augusta's 50th Anniversary: 1906–1956. Historical Panorama Program, John B. Rogers Producing Company, 1956.

Prather, Emily. *The Verderys of Georgia*. Atlanta: Williams Printing Company, 1942. Reprinted by Higginson Book Company.

Rowland, A. Ray and Helen Callahan. *Yesterday's Augusta*. Miami: E. A. Seamann Publishing, 1976.

Toole, Gaspar Loren II. *Ninety Years in Aiken County*. Aiken, SC: Self Published, 1957.